TAKEMUKI-GA-KI

Also by or translated by Royall Tyler

Fourteenth-Century Voices I

From the Bamboo-View Pavilion:
TAKEMUKI-GA-KI

by

Hino Nako

Translated by Royall Tyler

BLUE-TONGUE BOOKS

Charley's Forest NSW Australia

CONTENTS

This life is like a dream. Grant me, I humbly beg, aspiration to enlightenment and a happy rebirth. I long more and more to withdraw from the world. Vouchsafe true aspiration and turn my karma in this life to fortunate rebirth in the next. Confer upon Tadayoshi my present karma and keep him from harm.

Prayer by Ashikaga Takauji,
Kenmu 3.8.17 [1336]

How have you been since you went down from Kyoto? I worry, you know. Here, on 5.22, Akiie, the governor of Mutsu, was killed in Izumi, between Tennōji and Sakai. His head was presented for inspection. Miraculously, Hachiman and Sumiyoshi appeared, plainly visible, in the midst of the battle, and a good half-dozen ships lay burned out and sunk. Such was the gods' will. It filled me with hope for the future.

Uesugi Kiyoko, mother of
Takauji and Tadayoshi,
in a letter to one of them,
Engen 3.5.27 [1338]

Notes overleaf

(1) Takauji's prayer: *Dainihon shiryō*, series 6, vol. 3, *hoi*, p. 3. Although not to be taken literally, it expresses a pious medieval ideal. For a brief discussion, see Thomas D. Conlan, *State of War*, Center for Japanese Studies, University of Michigan, 2003, pp. 183-184.

(2) Uesugi Kiyoko's letter: *Nanbokuchō ibun*, Kantō-hen, vol. 1, no. 835 ("Uesugi Kiyoko shōsoku"), Tōkyōdō Shuppan, 2007, pp. 300-1. The recipient must have been one of her sons, probably Tadayoshi. Full text and translation at:

http://komonjo.princeton.edu/shoguns-mother/

The battle, *Ishizu no tatakai* (Engen 3.5.22), was fought on the shore at Izumi Sakai between Kitabatake Akiie and Takauji's chief lieutenant, Kō no Moronao.

PREFACE

This volume is the first of two entitled, together, *Fourteenth-Century Voices*. Tom Conlan started the project by suggesting that I translate *Baishōron*, an important account of critical developments in mid-century history. I tried, but the historical terrain was then too unfamiliar, and my attempt broke down. Fortunately, Shuzo Uyenaka generously granted us unrestricted use of the translation that he had made for his 1978 University of Toronto dissertation.

When *Baishōron* alone turned out to be short for a book, Tom, my wife Susan, and I considered further possibilities, especially first-person accounts. Susan suggested *Takemuki-ga-ki*, by Hino Nako. Tom's enthusiastic and learned support so propelled the work forward that, without him, *Fourteenth-Century Voices* would not exist. Thanks to him, Susan and I spent a semester at Princeton. By then the project had expanded so greatly that I decided to give *Takemuki-ga-ki* its own volume and put everything else in another. Susan did the layout, interior graphics, and covers for both, and also designed the imprint logo.

In introducing *Takemuki-ga-ki* in English (with the *Taiheiki* account of the death of Nako's husband and the birth of her son) I did not seek to address the wide audience reached more than forty years ago by the late Karen Brazell's remarkable translation of *Towazugatari*—a work written less than a decade before Nako was born. The texts in *Fourteenth-Century Voices* will appeal to a smaller audience, one more familiar with Japanese history, literature, and words.

The first section of *Takemuki-ga-ki* is dated 1329; the last ones datable are from 1349; and Nako (who, like Ashikaga Takauji, died in 1358) probably wrote her closing poems in 1350-1352. *Baishōron*, the first work in *Fourteenth-Century Voices II*, covers the same period from a different perspective. Neither mentions the Kannō Anarchy (*jōran*) of 1350-1352, summarized in the introduction to the second *Voices II*

1

text: the *Taiheiki* account of the Southern Court's abduction of the three Northern emperors, in 1352, to Anō in the Yoshino mountains. Nako knew one of these emperors, Kōgon, particularly well.

The third *Voices II* text, Nijō Yoshimoto's *Ojima no kuchizusami*, covers Emperor Go-Kōgon's flight from Kyoto to Mino, and his return, in 1353. Nako's son, Sanetoshi, who had grown up with Go-Kōgon, figures in it briefly.

The fourth *Voices II* text is the vivid *Gen'ishū* account, by an anonymous participant, of the crucial battle of Tōji in 1355. It refers twice to Imagawa Ryōshun, the author of the last two *Voices II* texts.

Kōgon renounced the world after his release from Anō in 1357. The fifth text, again from *Taiheiki*, evokes him as a wandering monk and describes his death (1364) at a temple in Tanba.

In *Michiyukiburi*, the sixth, Imagawa Ryōshun narrates his journey to Kyushu in 1371, charged by Ashikaga Yoshimitsu with quelling the Southern Court sympathizers there. Ryōshun's powerfully personal and historically valuable *Nantaiheiki*, the seventh, ends *Fourteenth-Century Voices II* in a manner worthy of the sequence begun by Hino Nako's unique memoir.

INTRODUCTION

Takemuki-ga-ki, by Hino Nako (1310?-1358), is the last of the twelve *joryū nikki* (diaries or autobiographical memoirs by women) written since the tenth-century *Kagerō nikki.* Fairly late in her life the author drew on notes and memories to compose a testament to the world that she had known and to her place in it. While some sections read at first glance like records of formal events, others are unmistakably personal. A few passages recall the *Pillow Book,* for example, but others are unlike anything else. Nako seems discreetly to have paced her entries, while maintaining roughly chronological order, so to achieve engaging or moving shifts of subject, perspective, and mood. At once sophisticated and genuine, *Takemuki-ga-ki* is a deeply distinguished work.

This introduction, translation, and accompanying apparatus rely on Iwasa Miyoko's *Takemuki-ga-ki zenchūshaku* (Kasama Shoin, 2011). Hino Nako often wrote in *demi-mot* allusions now identifiable only thanks to wide reading in such contemporary documents as *Hanazono-in shinki* or *Entairyaku*, among others, or to deep familiarity with her world and her work. So pervasive is Iwasa's contribution to this book that specific references to her research and findings, below, will be relatively few.[1]

Discovery and reception

The principal manuscript of *Takemuki-ga-ki*, held by the National Diet Library, probably dates from the early Edo period. Four others, elsewhere, are copies of it. Wada Hidematsu, who discovered the Diet

---

[1] This introduction relies above all on her *kaidai* (pp. 275-302). However, it also draws at times on the first chapter ("*Takemuki-ga-ki* no shūhen") of Itō Kei, *Shinhokuchō no hito to bungaku*, Miyai Shoten (Miyai sensho 6), 1979, pp. 2-51.

Library manuscript in 1910 and published it in 1911, called the work far inferior to earlier *joryū nikki*, dismissed it as little more than a manual for wives, and denied it literary value. Ikeda Kikan omitted it from his *Kyūtei joryū nikki bungaku* (1927), and Nagazumi Yasuaki called it, in his *Chūsei bungaku no tenbō* (1956), "the last dregs" of the genre.

In 1950 the publication of the recently-discovered *Towazugatari*[2] drew new attention to *Takemuki*. Tamai Kōsuke's "Takemuki ga ki," (*Gakuen*, January 1962) became the basic study of the work and its author. In a 1964 publication with the same title (*Nihon bungaku*, December), Tsukamoto Yasuhiko described it more sympathetically as "a faithful record of the feelings of a woman buffeted by the tempests of the time." Other studies followed. In 1990 the text (annotated by Iwasa) appeared in the *Chūsei nikki kikō shū* volume of the Iwanami *Shin Nihon koten bungaku taikei* series. Still, according to Iwasa, interest in and comprehension of the text proper (as distinguished from the enterprise of glossing discrete items) remains relatively low.[3] Imazeki Toshiko, who otherwise hardly mentioned *Takemuki*, expressed the same opinion in her recent volume of studies of such works.[4]

The difficulty is probably that *Takemuki* frustrates all assumptions about what a *joryū nikki* is or should be. How indeed to take, or to classify, a *joryū nikki* in which the emperor flees to a mountain fortress; in which one reigning and two retired emperors seek refuge at Rokuhara,[5] then flee when it burns down; in which fighting tears lover from lover; and in which the author's later profession of heartfelt religious faith springs from practice of Rinzai Zen? All this is quite apart from the *Taiheiki* account of how Nako saw her husband beheaded and bore his son in hiding. The entries in *Takemuki-ga-ki* take on depth and color from Nako's own words, of course, but even more from the dark ground against which they are to be read.

---

[2] Karen Brazell, tr., *The Confessions of Lady Nijō*, Stanford University Press, 1973.
[3] Iwasa, *Zenchūshaku*, p. 275.
[4] Imazeki Toshiko, *Kana nikki bungaku ron*, Kasama Shoin, 2013, pp. 13-14.
[5] The Kyoto headquarters of the Kamakura Bakufu.

Nako's name and the work's title

The name "Nako" is unusual enough to require comment. Some writers have cautiously read the characters "Meishi" instead.

Hanazono-in shinki (Genkō 1.10 [1331], *bekki*) refers to Nako as "Naishi-no-suke Sukeko" in connection with a ceremony that involved another Sukeko; and a line in the entry for Genkō 2.4.28 likewise mentions both her and a Sukeko described as a daughter of "the late Sukekiyo." Perhaps Nako's name was changed to avoid confusion with the other Sukeko; perhaps Hanazono did not know her personal name and so applied to her the first character of her father's, Sukena; or perhaps she received the second, *na* character of his name from the start. At any rate, as Donald Keene remarked, her name was certainly *not* read "Meishi."[6]

Nako wrote *Takemuki-ga-ki* on the Saionji Kitayama estate, where her Takemuki Pavilion looked out onto a bamboo grove. Since at Kitayama she would naturally have been referred to as "Takemuki," the title of her work means, approximately, "Nako's Memoir."

Nako's birth and lineage

In the court hierarchy of noble houses prevailing since early Kamakura times, the Hino counted as a *meika*, five steps down from the *sekke*, the houses from which a regent might be appointed. Below the *sekke* came, in descending order, the *seiga* houses, eligible for chancellor (*daijōdaijin*); the *daijinke* (minister); the *urinke* (grand counselor, *dainagon*); and, finally, the *meika*. In principle a *meika* scion, too, could rise to grand counselor, but his line was expected to specialize particularly in letters, Confucian studies, and *kojitsu*, the hallowed usages of the past.

Nako was therefore born far down in the highest division of the civil aristocracy: the one that produced senior nobles (*kugyō*). Her birth underlies her position at the start of *Takemuki* as a gentlewoman to Retired Emperor Go-Fushimi; her subsequent role as a dame of staff

---

[6] Donald Keene, *Seeds in the Heart*, New York: Henry Holt, 1993, p. 849, n. 54.

(*naishi no suke*); and above all the complexities surrounding her marriage to Saionji Kinmune (1310-1335). Already a grand counselor in his early twenties, Kinmune headed a house of *seiga* standing. In marrying Nako, he married down.

The Hino descended from Fujiwara no Uchimaro, the fourth son of Kamatari, the Fujiwara founder. During the Heian period the line produced mainly provincial governors. Two sons of Arikuni (sixth generation, 943-1011), became *bungaku hakase* ("doctor of letters"), and they and their descendants served as lower-level officials and tutors to emperors or heirs apparent. Sanemitsu (eleventh generation, 1069-1147) rose to the second rank and the office of acting counselor (*gon chūnagon*), the highest yet reached in the line. A nephew became the great Pure Land teacher Shinran (1173-1262).

Her family against the background of the Jimyōin-Daikakuji split

In the mid-13th century intense rivalry split the imperial succession into two lines: Jimyōin and Daikakuji. The solution imposed by the Kamakura bakufu (alternation every ten years) was collapsing when, in 1318, the Daikakuji emperor Go-Daigo came to the throne, intent on cutting off the Jimyōin line for good and bringing the bakufu down. In 1331 bakufu men surrounded the palace to arrest him.[7] However, he escaped and fled. Nako was present at the time and recorded the event, as well as the subsequent accession of the Jimyōin emperor Kōgon.[8] In 1333 Go-Daigo escaped again, this time from exile on the island of Oki; overthrew the Bakufu; deposed Kōgon; and instituted the "Kenmu Restoration." For decades thereafter two emperors claimed legitimacy in Japan: the Jimyōin, "Northern Court" emperor in Kyoto and the Daikakuji emperor of the "Southern Court."

[7] The Tominokōji palace (*dairi*), east of Tominokōji at the level of Nijō, built in 1317. By this time the formally planned imperial palace compound had fallen out of use after repeated fires. The Tominokōji palace was designed as a full replacement.
[8] Kōgon's later years as an influential retired emperor (*chiten no kimi*) have been called the last of the Kamakura-period government pattern, under which the court nobles retained a degree of autonomy (Ogawa Takeo, "Hokuchō teishin to shite no *Masukagami* no sakusha: seiritsu nendai, sakuzō no saikentō," *Mita bungaku* 32 [September 2000], pp. 13-14).

Jimyōin figures and interests formed Nako's personal world. Her grandfather, Hino Toshimitsu (1260-1326), served the Jimyōin emperor Fushimi and rose to acting grand counselor—a promotion that shocked many because of his relatively modest antecedents. His daughters became wetnurses to Go-Fushimi, Hanazono, and Kōmyō, all in the Jimyōin line. When Go-Daigo's son and heir apparent Prince Kuniyoshi died in 1326, Toshimitsu went to Kamakura and successfully had him replaced by the Jimyōin prince Kazuhito, the future Kōgon. He died in Kamakura a few months later.

Sukena[9] (1287-1338), Nako's father and Toshimitsu's son, likewise rose to grand counselor. He served Go-Fushimi, as did Nako in her early years. Daughters of his (not Nako) were wetnurses to Kōgon and Go-Kōgon. In 1333 he accompanied Kōgon in flight from Kyoto and renounced the world. A younger brother of his, Suketomo, joined Go-Daigo's plot to overthrow the Bakufu and was exiled to Sado. Another brother was the Shingon monk Kenshun, an influential Northern Court figure.[10]

Sukena's first wife (the daughter of a brother of his father) gave him four children: Nako, two sons, and, apparently, an older sister. The sister, perhaps four or five years older than Nako, married one Takatsukasa Fuyumasa. One brother, Fusamitsu, roughly two years older than Nako, accompanied Sukena, Kōgon, and the two retired emperors (Hanazono, Fushimi) on their flight from Kyoto in 1333 and renounced the world with his father.[11] Ujimitsu, five years younger, joined Nako's husband's plot against Go-Daigo and was executed in 1335. Nako mentions both.

Nako had half-siblings as well. Tokimitsu (1328-1367) followed his father as head of the Hino house. Nobuko (?-1382) was probably, like him, a child of Sukena's second wife, called in *Takemuki* "Shiba" or "Shiba no Zenni." In 1353 Nobuko played in Go-Kōgon's enthronement ceremony the same role (*kenchō*) as Nako's in that of Kōgon, in 1332

---

[9] For an discussion of Sukena's political activity, see Thomas D. Conlan, *From Sovereign to Symbol, Oxford University Press*, 2011, pp. 48-51.

[10] Studied by Conlan in *From Sovereign to Symbol* and discussed in the introduction to *Ojima no kuchizusami*.

[11] *Baishōron* covers this flight.

(no. 13). She seems to have been close to Yoshimitsu, and in 1381 she received the first rank. A third, presumably half-sister is recorded, whether reliably or not, as the "wife of the right minister Sanetoshi," Nako's son.

Her youth, with an analysis of her marriage

At the start of *Takemuki*, Nako is in her nineteenth year and a gentlewoman to Retired Emperor Go-Fushimi. Shortly before his accession (*senso*) two years later, Kōgon (Go-Fushimi's son) appointed her a dame of staff, presumably because her assigned ceremonial role (nos. 3, 13) required that title; but she seems to have returned to Go-Fushimi once the enthronement (*sokui*) was over. Her memoir suggests that she looked to Go-Fushimi above all and retained for him, even after his death (no. 53), a warmth of feeling absent from her remarks about Kōgon. She also knew Hanazono, who once teased her about seeming to be pregnant (no. 29).

Saionji Kinmune, Nako's future husband, headed a house that far outranked the Hino. How the two met is easily imagined, considering the close association between both and Kōgon. On Nako's side, family interests may have encouraged the relationship, and perhaps practical considerations counted for Kinmune as well. However, *Takemuki-ga-ki* leaves little doubt that they were in love. The marriage certainly served Kinmune's greater interests in the end. Not every wife could have so steadfastly and successfully supported the future of his son.

Nako's marriage is so interesting that Hitomi Tonomura devoted an essay to it and its place in the history of Japanese marriage practices.[12] Tonomura drew her account of the marriage from *Takemuki-ga-ki*, but Nako's brief allusions to the steps in the process are difficult to interpret without unusually profound familiarity with the work and its background. For that reason Iwasa Miyoko's reading of it is of special value.[13]

---

[12] "Re-envisioning Women in the Post-Kamakura Age." In Jeffrey P. Mass ed., *The Origins of Japan's Medieval World: Courtiers, Clerics, Warriors, and Peasants in the Fourteenth Century,* Stanford University Press, 1997.
[13] Iwasa, *Zenchūshaku*, pp. 292-295.

Iwasa credited Takamure Itsue's *Nihon kon'in shi* (Shibundō, 1963) with identifying the pattern that makes Nako's marriage process intelligible. Takamure called it *gisei mukotori kon* ("counterfeit matrilineal marriage"). Visible between the 1220s and the 1330s, it marks the transition from matrilineal (*mukotori kon*) to patrilineal (*yomeiri kon*) marriage.

Counterfeit matrilineal marriage upheld matrilineal marriage by fictionally assimilating the groom's home to the bride's. The form discernable in *Takemuki* followed these steps:

1. The bride's home receives the groom (*mukotori kon*).
2. For a time, the groom visits the bride there (*kayoi kon*).
3. The groom's parents then move out of their house or die.
4. At last the bride moves to the groom's family home as his wife.

In the case of Nako and Kinmune, the marriage begins as a secret affair. Kinmune takes Nako to Tokiwai House, the home of Retired Emperors Go-Fushimi and Hanazono (no. 25), and the two sleep together in an associated lodging. When Nako wrote, "I had found myself to my surprise spending nights away from home," she meant Tokiwai House.

The next year, on the first day of spring, Kinmune sends Nako a formal proposal of marriage (no. 26). A *mukotori kon* ceremony is then held at the Hino family home, where for a time Kinmune visits her (*kayoi kon*).

Kinmune's father, Saionji Sanehira, has passed away, and his widow lives in the city. Nako could move to this lady's residence as Kinmune's formal wife (*seishitsu*), but Kinmune wants her with him at Kitayama, the Saionji family estate. The matter therefore concerns the entire Saionji house. Some members object. A series of advantageous marriages over several generations had consolidated the Saionji position at court, but Nako offers no illustrious alliance. Being from a mere *meika*, in the eyes of the objectors she qualifies only as a mistress, not as a wife. For them, the wedding at the Hino residence does not count.

Kinmune therefore decides to have his uncle, the minister Saionji Suehira, adopt Nako and bring her to Kitayama as his daughter (no.

67). Then the Kenmu disaster intervenes. Kinmune despairs (no. 34). To keep him from renouncing the world, the Saionji bring Nako to Kitayama as his mistress, lodged well away from the main house in a temple on the estate (no. 33). At some point then Kinmune sees the way clear to resolve the matter. He returns Nako for a few days to her family home, then brings her back to Kitayama as his formal wife (no. 35).

The Saionji, Kitayama, and the death of Kinmune

The Saionji descend ultimately from Kinsue (957-1029), the tenth son of Fujiwara no Morosuke (908-960). Kinsue rose to chancellor, but the line yielded only grand counselors until Sanemune (1149?-1212), seven generations later, became palace minister (*naidaijin*). His son Kintsune (1171-1234), active at the start of the Kamakura bakufu, married a relative of Minamoto no Yoritomo and eventually became palace minister, then chancellor and *Kantō mōshitsugi* (court spokesman to the bakufu). He also amassed huge wealth from trade with Song China. Kintsune founded the Saionji line.

Masukagami (the "Uchino no yuki" chapter) describes as follows the origins of Kitayama and the Saionji name.

> The late Chancellor Kintsune...had been inspired by a dream to build a religious hall of unparalleled splendor, called the Saionji, in those same northern hills where the hero of *The Tale of Genji* went to seek a ritual cure for his chills and fevers. [He] had exchanged his Matsueda estate in Owari Province for the site, [which]...he had cleared, leveled, and transformed...into an elegant park, its every aspect in perfect taste—the densely forested hills, the vast lake, ample as a sea, and the waterfall plunging from the heights with a sound that evoked tears of emotion.[14]

The passage goes on to mention "the main hall of worship, the Saionji," with its magnificent Amida, and several other temples, including the

---

[14] George W. Perkins, tr., The Clear Mirror: *A Chronicle of the Japanese Court During the Kamakura Period (1185-1333)*, Stanford University Press, 1998, p. 72.

Myōon-dō that first sheltered Nako at Kitayama (no. 33), Muryōkō-in (no. 42), and Jōjūshin-in (no. 57).

Kintsune's successors—Saneuji (1194-1269), Kinsuke, and Sanekane—all served as chancellor and *Kantō mōshitsugi*, while their daughters married and bore emperors. It is Sanekane who, at the time of the Jimyōin-Daikakuji split, devised the plan to have the succession alternate between the two lines. Kitayama received frequent imperial visits.[15]

Sanekane was followed by Kinhira (1264-1315), Kinmune's grandfather. *Kantō mōshitsugi* like his forebears, Kinhira nonetheless stopped at the office of left minister, as Yoshida Kenkō noted with approval in *Tsurezuregusa* 83. His daughter, Go-Fushimi's empress, is the Kōgimon-in mentioned repeatedly in *Takemuki*. A lasting achievement of his was to commission *Kasuga Gongen genki* (1309), a beautiful picture-scroll account of the wonders performed by the deity of Kasuga, the Fujiwara ancestral shrine.[16] Nako mentions two visits to Kasuga (nos. 64, 70), and the name recurs in her memoir. She never actually quotes the *Genki* text, but her elaborate rhetoric in praise of the deity sounds so like it (and so unlike any passage of hers elsewhere) that one feels the strong family tie, now that she, too, is of Kitayama.

Kinhira's son Sanehira, the father of Kinmune, died in 1326. Kinmune therefore came very young to head the Saionji house. By 1331, the time of his first appearance in *Takemuki*, he was an acting grand counselor. He proposed to Nako early in 1333, and the steps outlined above followed. So did Go-Daigo's escape from Oki; the eastward flight of three (including Kōgon) retired emperors, accompanied by Nako's father and one of her brothers; and the fall of the Kamakura bakufu. Nako did not move formally to Kitayama until the sixth month, after the retired emperors' return. By then her father and one brother had renounced the world.

Two years or so later, in Kenmu 2.8. (1335), Nako was pregnant when Kinmune was arrested and executed for plotting to assassinate

---

[15] Sanekane is also the "Akebono," the author's lover, of *Towazugatari*,.

[16] Royall Tyler, *The Miracles of the Kasuga Deity*, Columbia University Press, 1990.

Go-Daigo. He had probably been betrayed by Kinshige, a half-brother seven years his junior.

Sanetoshi and the Saionji succession

Taiheiki tells how, after secretly bearing Sanetoshi, Nako feared that he might be found and killed. When Go-Daigo's Kenmu Restoration collapsed, he fled in 1336 to Yoshino. Kōmyō, Kōgon's full brother, then came to the Northern throne.

In 1337 Sanetoshi, in his second year, was formally admitted to the court.[17] He and his mother were then living in the Hino residence in the city, under the protection of Retired Emperor Kōgon, Eifukumon-in (Kōgon's adoptive grandmother), and Kōgimon-in (Kōgon's mother). At Kōgon's insistence they were soon joined there, despite the fire mentioned in no. 37, by Kōgon's month-old son, the future Go-Kōgon.

By 1340 Sanetoshi was the recognized head of the Saionji house. In that year Eifukumon-in, Fushimi's empress and a daughter of Saionji Sanekane, brought him to live near her at Kitayama (no. 41). Nako followed, and the Takemuki Pavilion at Kitayama became her home.

Nako wrote (no. 39), "Grave complications had arisen over the succession, but nothing came of them." She meant Kinshige's claim to the Saionji headship. He never gave it up, and her memoir alludes repeatedly to the struggle between his side and Sanetoshi's (hers). Kinshige became palace minster in 1349, and in 1352 he replaced Sanetoshi, who moved from Kitayama to the residence of Shiba no Zenni. The dispute was resolved only nine years after Nako's death. Kinshige's son Sanenaga having died young in 1355, Kinshige's death in 1367 extinguished his line.

---

[17] On Kenmu 4.10.8 (1337), in his third year, he was entered on the rank list (*joshaku*) at junior fifth rank, upper grade. On Ryakuō 2.1.5 (1339) he rose to full fifth rank, lower; on Ryakuō 3.8.2 to junior fourth, lower; on Kōei 1.1.5 (1342) to junior fourth, upper; and so on. He reached junior third rank on Kōei 3.1.5, in his tenth year. He was appointed a captain in the Left Palace Guards in Ryakuō 4 (1341) and, the next year deputy governor (*suke*) of Harima.

Last glimpses of Sanetoshi, Kitayama, and Kōgon

Sanetoshi had grown up with Go-Kōgon, whom he accompanied to Mino in 1353. He became acting grand counselor in 1358, the year of his mother's death; palace minister in 1364; and right minister in 1365. In 1375 he received the junior first rank, and in 1389 he died. His son (Nako's grandson) Kinnaga (1353-1390), a grand counselor at the time, was present when Ashikaga Yoshimitsu entertained Emperor Go-Enyū in 1381;[18] and it is his grandson Saionji Sanenaga (1377-1431) who, in 1397, sold Yoshimitsu the Kitayama estate, the future site of the Golden Pavilion.

Retired Emperor Kōgon, captured by the Southern Court early in 1352, returned to Kyoto in 1357 and renounced the world. The next year Nako, Ashikaga Takauji, Kōgimon-in, and Kōgon's empress Kianmon-in (nos. 43, 53, and later) all died. Kōgon, now a monk, passed away in 1364 at a temple in Tanba.

Painful times

Despite the dramatic events that she witnessed, Nako's early entries convey pride in the world she knew. After her husband's death and her move to Kitayama, that pride naturally shifted to her son, to the estate itself—the pride of the Saionji—and to the imperial figures who lived there or whose visits it received. However, the times continued to change. Nako wrote engagingly of pilgrimages and retreats, and unforgettably of faith (no. 56) and beauty (no. 57), but her *Takemuki-ga-ki* then often turns to deaths and memorials. Her next-to-last entry (no. 84) seems to have been written about 1349. Sanetoshi, then in his fifteenth year, would still have needed her.

Nako was a nun when she wrote her closing poems (no. 85), which probably date from about 1351. A glance at the madness of those years (the "Kannō Anarchy") suggests a ground against which to weigh her withdrawal from writing. She never mentioned Sanetoshi's loss of the

---

[18] Matthew Stavros, with Norika Kurioka, "Imperial Progress to the Muromachi Palace, 1381: A Study and Annotated Translation of *Sakayuku hana*," *Japan Review* 28 (2015), pp. 18, 32.

Saionji house to Kinshige; nor did she allude to the events of the Anarchy, summarized in the introduction to "The Northern Emperors' Journey to Anō, 1352" (*Fourteenth-Century Voices II*).

For whom did Nako write, and why?

Nako gave no reason for writing *Takemuki-ga-ki*. Early in the history of the work's modern reception it was suggested, for example, that she meant to enlighten her son on points of protocol and tradition; but no such explanation can account for what she actually wrote. For Iwasa Miyoko, Nako wrote *Takemuki* in response to an inner urge *("kaku kakaneba naranu" naishin no yōsei)*[19] that may have involved capturing in essence, for herself and her son, a life lived fully and well despite great trials. However, it may also be that she wrote in spirit for her husband. *Shinsenzaishū* (1364) includes a suggestive poem, the only one of hers selected for an imperial anthology:

> *wasureji yo ware dani hito no omokage o*
> *mi ni soete koso katami to mo seme*
> I will not forget. Yes, I will keep his portrait
> with me always to recall his presence."[20]

In the first of her two closing poems (no. 85) Nako speaks of having wasted her time in this world of sorrows foolishly collecting such scribblings, and in the second she hopes that her name will not suffer for her having done so. These are proper sentiments for anyone who has renounced the world; but no, Nako had not wasted her time. She had conveyed everything of which she wished to speak.[21]

---

[19] Iwasa, *Zenchūshaku*, p. 274.

[20] *Shinsenzaishū* 1603, by "The Mother of Gon-Dainagon Sanetoshi." The poem occurs in a series on the theme of *omokage*, which here means a portrait. The poem that follows it (by Gon-Chūnagon Kimio) says, "I will paint her portrait (*omokage o e ni kakite*) and keep it with me, even if this token (*katami*) little resembles her."

[21] It would be heartless to reproach Nako for not having described her husband's death. There is probably no point, either, in blaming the language then proper to women for having constrained her on such a subject. Horror might have constrained anyone, anywhere.

Costume and color, and abbreviations

Among the court nobility, costume amounted almost to a language that, like words, had to be spoken tastefully and correctly for the occasion; or that, like music, required discerning execution. It was fundamental to civilized life. Nako must have remembered tastefully accomplished dress fondly, and when she cited it, she must have done so with pride.

However, her many costume and color terms do not pass well into English. In the Penguin *Tale of Genji* I "translated" such terms nonetheless, despite suspecting all the while that I was hardly more than aligning on the page reassuringly familiar but not really helpful English words. In *Takemuki-ga-ki* these terms remain in romanized transcription and are explained in a glossary. Only colors are indicated, so as to give some purchase after all to the imagination. On these matters, I am indebted to Monica Bethe for her expert help.

In each section, titles like "His Majesty," "Retired Emperor," or "Heir Apparent" are spelled out at their first occurrence. However, to avoid cumbersome repetition they are then abbreviated "HM," "RE," "HA," and so on.

TAKEMUKI-GA-KI

BOOK ONE
1329 to mid-1333

1
Future Emperor Kōgon Comes of Age

Gentoku 1.12.28 [1329]. The Heir Apparent came of age and that night went to the palace,[22] where he stayed in the Anpukuden. The gentlewomen Jōrō, Nijō-dono, and Naishi attended him.[23] He and His Majesty [Go-Daigo] apparently met in the Hagi Room (*hagi no to*). Both had been kept busy rehearsing the complex protocol and procedure.

A diagram of the ceremony at the palace was to supplement the Retired Emperor's [Go-Fushimi's] diary.[24] The officials sent him one, but it was much too big, and I was asked to make it smaller. I had no idea how to do that, but somehow I managed to get everything onto a single sheet. He was very pleased and attached it to his diary. It is probably still there.

After the ceremony there was music at the RE's residence. The musicians were:

Rhythm	Fujiwara Counselor Fuyusada
Voice	Chamberlain and Left Gate Watch Officer Munekane
Shō	Nakanoin Former Grand Counselor Michiaki
Flute	Captain Norimune
Hichiriki	Nakanoin Consultant and Captain Chikamitsu
Biwa	The HA & the former Right Minister, Kikutei-dono
Sō-no-koto	Right Grand Controller Saneyo
Wagon	Acting Commissioner Fuyunobu

In the *ryo* mode they played *Ana tōto* and *Torinoha*, and, in *ritsu*, *Ise no umi*, *Manzairaku*, and *Santai no kyū*. That is all I could gather. I may well have some of it wrong.

---

[22] The Tominokōji palace.

[23] Here, as also in 2, 3, 7, 15, 27, and 30, Nako seems to treat as personal appellations for certain gentlewomen the terms *jōro*, *kōtō*, and *naishi* that properly designate a category or a title. A *jōrō* is a senior gentlewoman, and a *kōtō* is the most senior of the *naishi* ("staff women").

[24] Parts of this diary survive, but not Nako's reduced diagram, mentioned below.

Related Matters[25]

The heir apparent, Go-Fushimi's son Kazuhito (the future Emperor Kōgon, 1313-1364, r. 1331-1333), had come of age provisionally in 1322, but the formal ceremony planned for the next year was postponed. In 1324, when the Shōchū Incident weakened Go-Daigo's position, the Jimyōin side insisted that the throne should alternate between the Jimyōin and Daikakuji lines and demanded that Kazuhito be made heir apparent. This came to pass in 1326, after the previous heir apparent's unexpected death. This new status made Kazuhito's eventual coming-of-age (*genbuku*) rite in 1328 far more solemn than it would have been earlier. *Hanazono-in shinki* (Gentoku 1/11 & 12, *bekki*) covers the event in detail. Sukena, Nako's father, served the prince the ceremonial repast.

The ceremony was held in the palace. Go-Fushimi could not attend it because in this context an heir apparent was considered imperial and a retired emperor only a private individual. That is why Nako, who served Go-Fushimi, knew about the event only at second hand.

---

[25] Based on Iwasa, *Zenchūshaku*, pp. 5-7.

2
The Genkō Disturbance and Kōgon's Accession

On the night of 8.24 in Genkō 1 [1331], the Emperor [Go-Daigo] disappeared. The news spread at dawn on the 25th and provoked turmoil. The Retired Emperors [Go-Fushimi, Hanazono] went to Rokujō House,[26] since it was near Rokuhara, and the Heir Apparent shared their carriage. They were moved the next day to the Rokuhara North Pavilion.[27] The Emperor was rumored then to be on Mount Hiei,[28] but, actually, report had it that the eastern savages[29] were racing to Kasagi[30] because he had taken refuge there.

Meanwhile, the Court quickly raised with Kamakura the issue of the succession. When all was ready, on 9.2 the REs repaired from Rokuhara to Tsuchimikado House, where the new Emperor was to reside. They went straight home[31] after leaving instructions on how it was to be redone.

The accession (*senso*) took place on the 22nd. The event apparently required forty gentlewomen, but only thirty were available. The Mirror was present, but the Sword and Jewel were not back yet,[32] so the sword from the Day Room (*hiru no omashi*) served instead.

---

[26] Rokujō-dono, a residence of retired emperors since Go-Shirakawa, north of Rokujō and west of Nishinotōin. Rokuhara was the Kyoto headquarters of the Kamakura bakufu.

[27] A cypress-bark thatched building on the north side of the Rokuhara compound. *Masukagami* ("Murashigure") notes this move and mentions that the pavilion belonged personally to the Kamakura shoguns.

[28] The report that Go-Daigo had gone to Mt. Hiei was a ruse. According to *Taiheiki* 2 ("Shushō rinkō jitsuji ni arazaru ni yotte sanmon hengi no koto"), the Hiei monks soon discovered that the "emperor" was only Fujiwara no Morokata, a grand counselor. Morokata and two other courtiers then stole away to join Go-Daigo at Kasagi.

[29] *Azuma no ebisu*: Kamakura warriors. *Masukagami* ("Murashigure"), too, calls them *ebisu*.

[30] A hill (324 m.) that rises above the Kizu-gawa in the south of modern Kyoto-fu. Go-Daigo sought refuge at Kasagi-dera, the temple there.

[31] To Tokiwai House (Tokiwai-dono), the residence of Go-Fushimi and Hanazono, north of Ōinomikado and east of Kyōgoku.

[32] Go-Daigo had taken them with him to Kasagi.

On the 29th came news that Kasagi had fallen. An uproar greeted the previous Emperor's arrival at Rokuhara.[33] The Senior Nobles and Privy Gentlemen with him seem to have been lodged in one place or another. I shall write no more about that.

The fate of the Sword and Jewel was of pressing concern. When word reached His Majesty [Kōgon] that they were safe, every gentleman went to Rokuhara and accompanied them to the palace.[34] No words can describe the joy of the occasion. Two staff women, Kōtō and Hyōe, and I received them.[35] This must have been about the 10th of the 10th month.

Related Matters

Masukagami ("Murashigure"), *Taiheiki* 3, and *Kasagi engi* cover Go-Daigo's flight, as does *Baishōron*. Rokuhara men had surrounded the palace on the night of 8.24, but Go-Daigo escaped. *Masukagami* speaks of warriors turning the palace upside down in their frantic search for him.

On 8.25 Go-Daigo reached Tōnan-in at Tōdaiji, secured the allegiance of the Tōdaiji monks, then went on to Jubusenji, a Shingon and Hossō shugendō temple connected to Kōfukuji. The Kōfukuji monks themselves declined to support him. On 8.27 he reached Kasagi.

On 9.2 Rokuhara forces attacked Kasagi, and a few days later warriors set out from Kamakura. Fierce battles ensued. The temple burned, and Go-Daigo fled, disguised as a peasant. When captured he was taken to Eikyūji (now within Tenri-shi), a shugendō temple affiliated with Daigoji. Many others were captured at about the same time.

On 10.2 a Rokuhara contingent moved Go-Daigo to the Byōdōin and, the next day, to Rokuhara. On 10.9 the regalia in his possession were taken to the Chōkōdō (nos. 19, 44, 50), accompanied by Sukena, Nako's father, and other

---

[33] On 10.14 Go-Daigo was brought to the Rokuhara Southern Pavilion of Hōjō Tokimasa.

[34] According to *Hanazono-in shinki*, they reached Rokuhara on 10.6.

[35] Nako is now Kōgon's dame of staff (*naishi-no-suke*).

nobles. They were ceremonially conveyed to the palace on 10.13.

Taiheiki and *Masukagami* state that Go-Daigo had taken all three regalia. However, *Hanazono-in shinki* for 10.6 and elsewhere mentions only the Sword and Jewel, and Nako's testimony is even more explicit. The Sword and Jewel were accessible to a fleeing emperor, but the Mirror was kept elsewhere, under guard.

3

The Sword and Jewel

On the 13th His Majesty [Kōgon] repaired to the palace surrounded by guards, while crowds filled the streets. That evening, handsomely outfitted retainers, servants, and oxherds escorted me to the palace. Sanmi-dono[36] accompanied me, and one gentlewoman also shared our carriage. The rest rode in my uncle's carriage.[37]

While we waited for HM in the Morning Room (*asagarei*), His Excellency the Right Minister[38] came and taught us how to hold the Sword and Jewel. I wore:

uragiku no itsutsuginu, hyōmon ari	white, with pattern
	white
	yellow
	ao green
	ao green
kurenai no hitoe	scarlet
urayamabuki no karaginu, hyōmon	yellow over scarlet
suzushi no hakama	

The staff women—Kōtō bearing the Sword and Hyōe the Jewel—proceeded to the gentlewomen's sitting room (*daibandokoro*), where I came forward to receive both at the sliding-panel entrance (*shōji guchi*). I laid them in the two-tiered cabinet (*nikai*) in the Night Chamber (*yoru no otodo*) and covered them with glossed purple silk.

The wrapping and cords of the Jewel's case were torn and worn badly enough to threaten a mishap. A decision was reached on the spot to rewrap it. The Regent [Takatsukasa Fuyunori] ordered the materials, which must have come from the Storehouse Office (*kuraryō*). The wrapping cloths were *ko-aoi* damask and glossed *moegi* silk with a *yanagi* lining, and the cord was dark purple. I did the wrapping and tying on the dais (*daishōji*) in the Morning Room, *en déshabillé*.[39] His

---

[36] Probably her grandmother Hiroko, the wife of Hino Toshimitsu.

[37] "The *bettō*'s carriage": that of Yanagihara Sukeaki, Toshimitsu's son. The title *bettō* presumably refers to his later appointment, in 1336, as chief of the imperial police.

[38] Koga Nagamichi.

[39] *Hadaka ginu. Hadaka* ("unclothed") means that the woman is not wearing something that she would normally wear, such as *mo*, *karaginu*, or *uchiki*. Nako has on only *kosode*, *hakama*, and *hitoe*; anything less would slight the Jewel. In 17th c. France

Lordship watched and showed me how. The cord goes around all six sides of the box in a fine lattice pattern. The original cord was neat and tight, but mine was slack and stretched when tugged. I had to keep it perfectly taut, which was very difficult. I might not even remove my sleeves or roll them up, and that made the work quite frustrating. The box was black lacquer, worn dull. There were locked clasps on one side. During the Heike wars the Treasure Sword remained in the sea; only the Jewel floated and returned to the capital. It was extraordinary to be able to handle so freely an object that has come down to us from the Age of the Gods.

te ni naruru	An honor, that was,
chigiri sae koso	to handle with such freedom
kashikokere	just once in my life
kamiyo furinuru	the guardian of our sovereigns
kimi ga mamori wa	since the Age of the Gods!

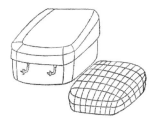

Hanazono's drawing of the jewel case
(*Hanazono-in shinki,* reproduced in Iwasa, *Zenchūshaku,* p. 19)

In the room next to the Night Chamber, the staff women (*naishi*) and the Dame of Staff[40] took turns attending the Sword and Jewel.

Genjō is properly stored in a cabinet (*zushi*) in the Morning Room, but in these worrying times it rests in a two-tiered cabinet (*nikaidana*) in the Night Chamber, covered with purple silk.[41] I never touched it without wearing a train.

---

the expression "en déshabillé" could describe a woman wearing an ample skirt that trails behind her on the ground and a top with elbow-length sleeves that ends in a flounce at her waist.

[40] Nako herself.

[41] The venerable biwa Genjō figures in *setsuwa* stories and in the Noh play *Genjō*. It was almost one of the regalia.

The pair of cabinets in the room where HM spends most of his time[42] are larger than usual. They have delicate, applied patterns cut from gold foil, with roundels of birds, flowers, and so on in powdered silver and gold, and polished mother-of-pearl gingko leaf designs. The Hagi Room furnishings are decorated with paulownia, bamboo, and phoenixes. The cabinet in the Ninjuden has Chinese pictures on it.[43] All glitter and gleam beautifully. The late Left Minister and Chikurin-in Novice [44] chose these pieces of furniture himself, and he certainly did not do so half-heartedly. Even things like the poles (*sao*) for hanging robes, in the gentlewomen's rooms, were very pretty.[45]

Related Matters[46]

Kōgon seems to have made Nako a dame of staff (*naishi no suke*) shortly before his accession, precisely in order to qualify her for this role.[47] Her service name was Chūnagon-no-naishi, Sukena having served previously served as a counselor.

Hanazono-in shinki (Genkō 10.13, *bekki*) covers Kōgon's move to the Tominokōji palace in detail. Hanazono and Go-Fushimi watched the procession from their carriage (or carriages), but they had inspected the palace the day before and made sure that the two *naishi* (Kōtō and Shōshō) knew how to handle the sword and jewel.[48]

---

[42] The north aisle (*kitabisashi*) of the Seiryōden.
[43] Paintings of lions, tigers, and other such exotica.
[44] Saionji Kinhira (1264-1315), Kinmune's grandfather.
[45] The Tominokōji palace had been built largely by Kinhira, who also commissioned *Kasuga Gongen genki*, but it remained unfinished when he died. Saionji Sanekane completed it. Its beauty impressed Hanazono, too (*Shinki* for Bunpō 1.3.20).
[46] Derived from Iwasa, *Zenchūshaku*, pp. 18-20.
[47] In the world of *Genji monogatari*, four *naishi-no-suke* served under a *naishi-no-kami*. By Nako's time, a *naishi-no-kami* appointment was very rare, and there seems to have been only one *naishi-no-suke* at a time. See Wakita Haruko, *Women in Medieval Japan*, translated by Alison Tokita, Clayton: Monash Asia Institute and Tokyo: University of Tokyo Press, 2006, p. 167.
[48] In *Nakatsukasa-no-naishi nikki* the regent, Morotada, tells the author in connection with the accession of Go-Fushimi that the best way to carry the jewel case is to slip one's fingers under the web of cords around it.

One might imagine that the damage repaired by Nako occurred at Dan-no-ura or Kasagi, but apparently not. The jewel case was rewrapped during Einin [1293-1298], during Shōan [1299-1301], and again in Ōchō 2 [1312] (*Hanazono-in shinki* for Ōchō 2.2.3). Even in ordinary times it seems to have been subject to wear.

4
An Eclipse of the Sun

On the 1st of the 11th month there was an eclipse of the sun. It had snowed a lot during the night, and His Majesty was so annoyed to be curtained off[49] that the Saionji Grand Counselor [Kinmune] confined himself with him. I heard that HM had the upper chamber[50] opened a little, peeked out, and then emerged with his entourage. Being shy and retiring, I did not rise immediately but remained near the brazier. "What is this?" the Grand Counselor exclaimed. "Why, she must be afraid of the snow!" and so on. It was quite amusing. Afterwards I went out for a look. The bamboo in the bed outside was already bent over under the weight of snow, and the fire hut,[51] too, was almost buried. It was all extremely pretty.

His Majesty sent Eifukumon-in[52] a letter on thin, *momiji* paper tied to a bamboo sprig from the edge of the bed. The messenger managed to keep the snow from falling off it.

One brilliantly moonlit night HM set out with some of his gentlewomen toward the Chamberlains' quarters (*kurōdo no machi*). We had a lovely, distant view of the Anpukuden and Left Gate Watch headquarters, and we heard voices singing the closing anthem[53] in the Takiguchi Guards' lodge. The voices calling "Omaetachi!" were great fun. We wandered about here and there singing songs, and the very crunching of our shoes against the ground seemed to ring bright and clear to the heavens.

---

[49] During a solar eclipse the emperor remained confined in the palace, which was wrapped in matting lest light from the eclipse strike the imperial person. After noting three inches of snow that day, Hanazono called the eclipse a "fortunate portent" at the start of a new reign and "highly significant."

[50] Iwasa, *Zenchūshaku*, p. 21 describes this space, which indeed gave onto a bamboo bed (*take no dai*).

[51] *Hitakiya*, where the guards kept a fire (*kagaribi*) going in a sort of iron basket (a cresset).

[52] Fujiwara no Shōshi, a daughter of Saionji Sanekane, Emperor Fushimi's empress, and Kōgon's adoptive grandmother. She lived at Kitayama.

[53] *Kaeriasobi*, possibly the felicitous words (*shūgen*) sung after the roll call (*nadaimen*). The meaning of *omaetachi*, below, is unknown. Perhaps it is a "Who goes there?" challenge.

5
The Special Kamo Festival

In the 11th month the special (*rinji*) Kamo festival was held at the palace.[54] Once the purification (*gokei*) was over, His Majesty sat in his chair by the aisle (*hisashi*) blinds. He summoned the Head Chamberlain and Senior Nobles, who took their seats on the long bridge (*nagahashi*).[55] The envoys and others[56] came in through the Takiguchi entrance and seated themselves on the ground. The nobles drank[57] and gave them, too, wine. The cup went round and round. The Senior Nobles put

made-up flowers (*kazashi*) in the envoys' and dancers' hair,[58] then took their seats on the veranda (*sunoko*). When it was over, the light from the outdoor fires died out, and the return began. Dawn lit up the clouds trailing above the hills, and the dancers' *yama-ai* green sleeves looked limp.[59] As day came on HM, seated in his chair wearing *hiki nōshi* and ceremonial accessories, looked more impressive than ever. The sleeves continued visibly to wilt amid passing flurries of snow.

Pattern on a dancer's costume

---

[54] The date should have been 11.26, but no other document mentions the event.

[55] Between the Seiryōden and the Shishinden.

[56] The imperial envoys to the Kamigamo and Shimogamo Shrines, together with the dancers and musicians.

[57] *Kenpai*, a drink before the ceremony begins.

[58] Ministers gave the envoys wisteria clusters, while other nobles gave the dancers cherry blossoms.

[59] They had been starched. The participants are wearing *omigoromo*.

yuki ya nao	Will snow upon snow
kasanete samuki	redouble the cold of dawn,
asaborake	as in the palace court
kaesu kumoi no	the dancers still toss their sleeves,
yama-ai no sode	pattern-dyed with *yama-ai*?

6

Snow at the Palace

The year was nearly over when, on the last day of the horse [Genkō 1.12.29, 1331] I went to the Council of State Office (*kan no chō*)[60] in my capacity as Dame of Staff, to assist at the Burning of the Hair (*ogushi-age*).[61] It was an unpleasant night with a strong wind, and I kept my face buried in my clothes all the way there. "Look at this snow!" I heard someone say. "It's really coming down!" The remark startled me, and I peeked out. Yes, there was some on the ground already, and soon it was quite deep. In that setting it made everything so much more beautiful that I wished I had someone to enjoy it with.

furinikeru	Falling age on age,
yoyo o kasanete	snow on snow, reign after reign
ōuchi ya	has graced the palace
ikue tsumoreru	ah, how many joyous times
miyuki naruran	with each new sovereign's coming?[62]

---

[60] One of the buildings remaining in the old palace grounds, still used on formal occasions.

[61] The emperor's and heir apparent's hair clippings for the year were burned at the Bureau of Grounds (*Tonomoryō*), a palace facility where palanquins, gardening brooms & rakes, curtains, lamps, and other such paraphernalia were kept.

[62] The poem plays on *miyuki*, "imperial progress" and a noble word for "snow." This double meaning will recur below.

7
Kagura at the Naishidokoro

On the 28th His Majesty attended kagura at the Naishidokoro.[63] I was there in my capacity as Dame of Staff. I wore:

itsutsuginu, kōbai no nioi	progressively shaded plum pink, over
masaritaru hitoe	darker pink, under
kurenai no uchiginu	scarlet, under
moegi no uwagi	grass green, under
akairo no karaginu	red

I carried an open fan.

The staff lady (Kōtō) wore

yanagi no [itsutsu]ginu	white over ao green, under
kurenai no hitoe	scarlet, under
uchiginu, also kurenai	scarlet, under
ebizome no karaginu	grape purple

The staff maid (*toji*)[64] held the sacred streamers (*mitegura*) forth to the staff lady, who took them and passed them to the Dame of Staff (me), who then presented them to HM. After performing the salutation (*gohai*), HM moved to his seat at the edge of the room. The fresh matting laid for the occasion conveyed deep sanctity. The cressets outside lit up the lead dancers beautifully. As dawn approached the music seemed to ring more clearly than ever through the heavens, and somehow this poem came to me:

itodo nao	More brilliantly still
kumoi no hoshi no	ring out over the palace
koe zo sumu	voices singing "Morning Star,"
ame no iwato no	while the Celestial Rock Cave
akuru hikari ni	releases the light of dawn.

---

[63] The Unmeiden room where the sacred mirror was kept, guarded by staff ladies (*naishi*). Kagura was performed annually, on an auspicious day in the 12th month, in the west court of the Unmeiden. *Hanazono-in shinki* dates this event to the 17th.

[64] A *naishidokoro* servant.

8
New Year Rites

The New Year came, and spring glory renewed the splendor of the palace. Well might all exchange serene glances. The Salute to the Four Directions (*shihōhai*) took place at first light.[65] His Majesty proceeded out through the third southward span of the Seiryōden, the lattice shutters of which had been raised; and there in the court he performed the Salutation, surrounded by the Taisō screens.[66] The sword-bearer attended him to the south, and the shoe-bearer[67] to the west. For the Lesser Morning Salutation (*kochōhai*)[68] the blinds along the Seiryōden aisle were raised and those of the chamber (*moya*) lowered. The Regent then lifted the blinds to allow HM to come forth. HM seated himself on his chair in the second span from the north, and through the east door of the Privy Chamber watched the privy gentlemen enjoy their wine.[69] The gentlewomen served him with their *hitoe* skirts over their heads (*suso-kazuki*).

During the first three days of the year, gentlewomen served HM his festive repast (*baizen*) in the Morning Room.

---

[65] At the hour of the tiger, in the open area east of the Seiryōden, the emperor salutes the four directions, Ise first.

[66] A pair of six-fold screens depicting Chinese people playing a game known as *dakyū*.

[67] The former is Right Captain Fujiwara no Sanetsugu, the latter Left Grand Controller Fujiwara no Nagamitsu.

[68] On the first morning of the year the court officials, from imperial princes down to gentlemen of the sixth rank, lined up in the open space east of the Seiryōden to salute the emperor.

[69] *Ensui*, wine generously enjoyed on the first day of the year, in the emperor's presence.

9

The Imperial Visit to Kitayama

The second day was setsubun (*haru no sechi*),[70] and the directional taboo (*katatagae*) brought His Majesty and both Retired Emperors to Kitayama. Their rooms were done up to receive them. In HM's a full *nōshi* set hung on garment racks (*ika*). A sword and biwa awaited each in a purple bag with gold (*kinran*) patterning. A set of *Kokinshū* scrolls, too, was there in its box, likewise wrapped in gold-patterned purple, and with hand-made pine sprigs tied to each end with fine cord. The gifts set out on the dining tray (*daiban*) consisted of stones made from various materials and covered with a *hitoe* of *suzushi*.[71]

To the Senior RE [Go-Fushimi] went the Takemuki pavilion, where a complete set of clothing hung on a rack:

> *kariginu, kō no neri usumono*   light orange
> *aya no hitoe*
> *sashinuki*
> *shita no hakama*

There were also a cypress fan (*hiōgi*) and a sash (*obi*).

Her Retired Majesty[72] was given the Kogosho. She received:

> *mittsu onzo hakubai no futae orimono, yaezakura no eda o uchiokite*
> *murasaki no usuku koku o oru; hana wa shiro ukite oru*
>> triple *uchiki* set, double-layered *hakubai*, with double-petaled cherry branches bearing white, weft-float blossoms, on a light-to-dark purple ground
> *usu onzo [uchiki], kōbai no kataorimono*   plum pink
> *hakama*

The Ko-kugyōza[73] went to the Junior RE [Hanazono]. The rack was too far back in the room for me to see what hung on it. I gathered that Tsuneyasu had placed it there.[74] The drinking went on all night. HM

---

[70] The formal start of spring, normally associated with directional taboos (below).

[71] These gifts acknowledge the rare privilege of an imperial visit and the eternity of the reign. They are derived from *Shūishū* 299, a poem related to the Japanese national anthem: "In our sovereign's reign, the celestial feather mantle rarely descends to brush the rocks below: unworn, they endure."

[72] Kōgimon-in, Kōgon's mother.

[73] Unknown, but obviously a room suitable for an exalted personage.

[74] Takakura Tsuneyasu, Right City commissioner, third rank. His line specialized in

had been due to return at dawn, but it was broad day by the time he left.

dress.

10
What the Gentlewomen Wore for the New Year

The gentlewomen wore full ceremonial dress[75] during the first three New Year days, but on the fourth they appeared *en déshabillé*, and on the fifth in light dress (*usuginu*) as though at home (*uchiuchi sugata*). Those allowed the forbidden colors seem to have worn double robes.[76] Dress on the seventh and fifteenth was *en déshabillé*. During those fifteen days most visitors wore a fivefold set (*itsutsuginu*). Senior gentlewomen (*jōrō*) and the Dames of Staff (*suketachi*)[77] sat in the Morning Room. The more junior gentlewomen, down to the lowest among them, remained in the gentlewomen's sitting room (*daibandokoro*). The chamber-pot handlers (*hisumashi*) went about all dressed up, and it was fun to see the guards, Takiguchi and others, strutting by. They came up to the palace almost every day to call on their lady friends.

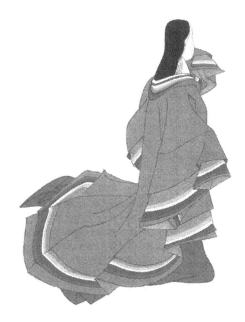

---

[75] *Mo* and *karaginu*.
[76] These would have been *uchiki*.
[77] This is the only suggestion in the work that there might be more than one dame of staff at a time.

11
The Special Festival at Iwashimizu

The 13th of the 3rd month brought the Yawata Special (*rinji*) Festival.[78] It began at the hour of the monkey [4 p.m.]. Her Retired Majesty[79] [Kōgimon-in] watched from the Ninjuden. Her standing curtain (*kichō*) was allowed to spill out past the blinds. The two central Seiryōden bays (*ken*) were opened, and the gentlewomen watched from there.

The Imperial Envoy was the Horikawa Consultant Captain.[80] The dancers and musicians were as usual.[81] The Senior Nobles included:

The Sanjō Grand Counselor [Fujiwara no Sanetada]
The Saionji Grand Counselor [Kinmune]
The Regent's Grand Counselor [Takatsukasa Morohira, the regent's son]
The Sochi Counselor [Bōjō Toshizane]
The Tokudaiji Counselor [Kinkiyo]
The Tominokōji Counselor Captain [Kinnobu].

The Horikawa Grand Counselor[82] joined them in a private capacity, in order to support his son. At nightfall the procession left through the North Gate. His Majesty and Her Retired Majesty watched from the Black Door (*kuroto*) gallery. I heard that off toward Kyōgoku one of the dancers fell when his horse bolted. Lords Tokudaiji and Horikawa attended HM. The flowers offered from hither and yon were sent floating down the palace brook and kept coming until dark.[83] They looked very pretty.

---

[78] The Iwashimizu Hachiman *rinji matsuri* began in Tengyō 5 (942) and occurred on the middle day of the horse in the 3rd month.

[79] Neishi, a daughter of Saionji Kinhira, Go-Fushimi's empress, mother of future Emperor Kōmyō, and honorary mother (*junbo*) of Hanazono.

[80] Minamoto no Tomomasa, in his thirteenth year.

[81] An unintelligible five-character phrase that follows this sentence may refer to the time of day.

[82] Minamoto Tomochika, Tomomasa's father.

[83] No record of this practice occurs elsewhere.

12

The Emperor Announces His Enthronement at the Office of Shrines

On the 16th His Majesty repaired to the Office of Shrines in order to offer *mitegura* and announce[84] his formal enthronement (*sokui*). Those due to appear pleaded various impediments (*sawari*) to be absent, and no one attended him. The Senior Nobles present were, among others, the Ōinomikado Grand Counselor and the Right Watch Intendant.[85] His palanquin was carried in through the north gate of the Office of Shrines and set down on a mat in the open space before the building. A single Staff Lady preceded it. She alighted from her carriage before the gate, continued on from there along a mat-covered path, and awaited him within the double doors (*tsumado*), her hair lifted high over her forehead.[86] HM's palanquin arrived. Attended by the Regent, he then seated himself on a dais (*daishōji*). The Staff Lady placed the Sword and Jewel to his left.

A white silk cloak had come in a Chinese chest (*karabitsu*) from the Imperial Stores. HM donned it, seated on the cushion provided.[87] He then put on an unpatterned headdress. Grand Counselor Fuyunobu helped to dress him, with the assistance of Norikata.[88] The Chinese accessories box (*karakushige*) arrived. HM then seated himself on the dais. The Grand Counselor tied the thin, *suzushi* snood (*koji*) on for him. The Chamberlain Captain[89] presented the black-lacquered pitcher (*hanzō*) and basin (*tarai*), as well as the toothpick (*yōji*) and the hand towel (*tanagoi*) in a willow box (*yanaibako*) placed on a stemmed tray (*takatsuki*). The basin had a woven bamboo cover (*nukisu*). HM rinsed his hands; moved eastward from his dais onto the square mat (*hanjō*) laid there for him; faced west; and summoned his personal attendant (*toneri*). The members of the Office of Shrines (*jingikan*) received their

---

[84] To Ise.

[85] Fujiwara Fuyunobu and Aburakōji Takakage.

[86] As normal for a gentlewoman in formal circumstances. It was secured with long hairpins.

[87] *Hirashiki*: a round cushion (*shitone*) centered on two parallel mats with the brocade *ungen* border reserved for a reigning emperor.

[88] Takakura Norikata, a chamberlain and the governor of Nagato, a costume specialist.

[89] Sanjō Sanetsugu.

mitegura and withdrew, each according to his own protocol.[90]

---

[90] Jingikan officials belonging the Ōnakatomi, Inbe, and Urabe houses received *mitegura* (also *gohei*) to offer to Amaterasu. The procedure differed for each.

13
Preparations for the Enthronement

The enthronement took place on the 22nd of the month. Having been assigned to lift the curtain,[91] I retired the previous day to my Aburanokōji home—one so beautifully appointed, I felt, that it really was a "glittering palace" (*tama no utena*).[92] For my return to the palace they stood a four-foot screen against the blinds in the chamber of the main house. My palm-leaf (*biryō*) carriage was drawn up to the portico (*higakushi*). (They laid a plank for me and put up a screen.) Once the yin-yang master's purification (*henbai*)[93] was over I boarded it,[94] assisted by Fusamitsu.[95] I wore:

tsubomi kōbai no itsutsuginu	plum pink over grape purple
aoki hitoe	ao green
akairo no karaginu	red
suzushi hakama	

The gentlewoman who rode behind me wore:

kōbai no nioi [no itsutsuginu]	shaded plum pink
masaritaru hitoe	deeper pink
moegi no uwagi	moegi green
akairo no karaginu	red
stencil-dyed train	

Her skirts spilled forth on high display from the right rear of the carriage.[96] Two outriders (*saki*) and housemen (*saburai*) almost beyond counting accompanied my procession. A display carriage (*idashi-guruma*) is properly brought up to the end of a wing (*tai*), but, because of all the display silks, mine were brought up to the secondary carriage dock

---

[91] The curtain surrounding the Takamikura was lifted on the left side by a lady of imperial lineage (*joō*) and on the right by a dame of staff. The office was called *kenchō*.
[92] The Hino mansion built by her grandfather, Toshimitsu, at Aburakōji and Nakanomikado.
[93] An incantation (*juhō*) performed when a distinguished person left or returned, to ward off evil spirits.
[94] *Izari-noru*: she slides along the plank on her knees and shins.
[95] Her elder brother.
[96] *Takadashi*: not from under the rear blind, but from between it and the handhold to one side.

(*kuruma-yose*) of the main house. The silks were high-displayed from the front only:

The first display carriage:

On the left

kōbai no nioi itsutsuginu	five plum pink layers, each darker
masaritaru hitoe	still darker plum pink
yamabuki no karaginu	yellow, scarlet-lined
ebizome no uwagi	grape purple
kurenai no uchibakama	scarlet
kaifu no mo	seashore train

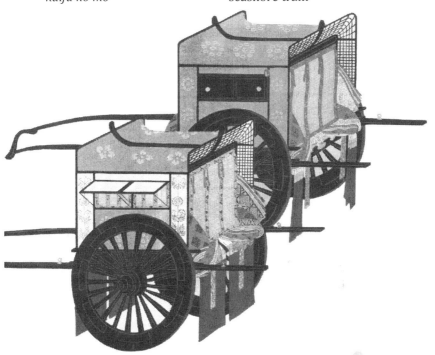

Display carriages

On the right

matsugasane [itsutsuginu]	two *suō* maroon layers, dark over light
	three *moegi* green, darker to lighter
kurenai no hitoe	scarlet
uchiginu (kurenai)	scarlet
kōbai no uwagi	plum pink
uchibakama	
ebizome no karaginu	grape purple
kaifu no mo	seashore train

41

The second display carriage:

On the left

murasaki no usuyō [itsutsuginu]	three purple layers, each lighter
	two white
shiroki hitoe	white
kurenai no uchiginu	scarlet
hakama	
yamabuki no uwagi	yellow
moegi no karaginu	grass green

On the right

yanagi [no itsutsuginu]	fivefold *yanagi* green
kurenai no hitoe	scarlet
uchiginu (kurenai)	scarlet
kōbai no uwagi	plum pink
ebizome no karaginu	grape purple

All displayed the train sash. The page girls (*warawa*) and maids (*shimozukai*) followed discreetly in whatever other carriages were available.

They readied a plank at my curtained enclosure (*yasumaku*) and brought my carriage up to it.[97] Our display silks should properly have spilled out through the second and third bays from there, but so many page girls and maids were crowded into the third one, dressing, that we could put them out no further than the second; our display from the third was a mere token. A strong wind was blowing the standing curtains back into the room, and it was only with some difficulty that we managed to get our silks out at all. They brought in my cabinet[98] and other furnishings (*chōdo*), placed them, stood a five-foot screen against the wall. There was a wall curtain (*kabeshiro*).[99] In the third bay they put a lunch box (*hiwarigo*) on a three-tiered set of shelves. The female menials (*binjo*) sat on low benches (*shōji*), wearing:

moegi no akome, hyōmon ari	grass green with pattern
kōbai no hitoe	plum pink
shiroki mo	white train

---

[97] Her curtained space, to wait in, is on the north side of the east-west gallery of the Council of State headquarters.

[98] From her own home.

[99] Hung from an overhead beam, in place of a wall.

In due course a messenger announced that it was time to enter the presence, so we got ready.[100] All wore:

kurenai no kinu, kazu muttsu	sixfold scarlet layering
hitoe (kurenai)	scarlet
uchiginu	
hakama	
moegi no uwagi	grass green
akairo no karaginu	red
jizuri no mo	stencil-dyed train

My special assistant (*tokusen*)[101] from Personal Furnishings (*mizushi-dokoro*) brought in ceremonial wear (*reifuku*). I changed into it from my *karaginu* and *mo*. The thing is to leave the sides open and loose, and to tie the train tight around the waist. She also brought me a *hitai*.[102]

When the time came I lifted my hair and opened my fan. Nii (Yanagi-dono) and Sanmi (Matsu-dono), as well as the Junior Retired Emperor's [Hanazono's] Chūnagon no Sanmi,[103] Horikawa, and Saishō-no-suke accompanied me and seemed prepared to assist me as required. Before us went two page girls, the one on the left bearing the incense burner (*hitori*) and the one on the right the cushion (*shitone*). They wore:

kōbai no kazami	plum pink
murasaki no mittsu akome	purple
shiroki hitoe, kumo wo tsuku	white with cloud pattern
kurenai no uchiginu	scarlet
hakama	
moegi no ue no hakama	grass green
ka ni arare	
uwazashi, murasaki no nioi	purple shaded dark to light

---

[100] The author and presumably her gentlewomen. They put up their hair (that is, built it up high above their foreheads) and opened their fans.

[101] *Tokusen* were specially chosen *uneme* (palace serving women) appointed to the Office of Personal Furnishings. The author and the other *kenchō* appointee each had one.

[102] A hair ornament for the front of the head (*maegami*), held in place by three hairpins (*saishi*). The meaning of the remark on how to wear the ceremonial robe is uncertain.

[103] Fujiwara no Kageko, Hanazono's dame of staff. The others mentioned remain unidentified.

43

monoimi, kurenai no usuyō	scarlet

They held open fans. So many distinguished privy gentlemen had provided fans, in such numbers, that in the end there were too many.

I proceeded to where the rite was to take place, surrounded by the joined panels of four standing curtains.[104] Four Privy Gentlemen held them: Fusamitsu, Ujimitsu, Tomomitsu, and Munemitsu.[105] Two attendants followed me, wearing:

yanagi no mittsuginu	three *yanagi* green layers
kōbai no hitoe	plum pink
uchiginu	
hakama	
ebizome no karaginu	grape purple
kaifu no mo	seashore train
monoimi and fan as for page girls	

Next came six *suso-kazuki* attendants:[106]

suzushi no hakama, soba o hasamu[107]

usuginu

orimono

enuimono

---

[104] The curtains screen the author from sight.

[105] The first two are the author's brothers, the second two her cousins.

[106] Women attendants with their *hitoe* skirts over their heads.

[107] The side(s) of the *hakama* tucked into the waistband.

To the right of the Takamikura[108] was a bench. I sat on a cushion placed upon it. I gathered that the other bench should properly be southwest of the Takamikura,[109] but actually it was due west. Perhaps this had been the special assistants' idea. I wonder which position is right. The page girls and attendants stopped outside the tall double doors (*takatsumado*).[110]

---

[108] The Japanese counterpart of the sovereign's throne: an elaborately roofed, open-sided, hexagonal structure resting on an ornamented dais. A divided curtain covers the south-facing side. The author and her colleague were each to lift one half of the curtain (or at least go through the motions of doing so; see note below), thus revealing the new emperor.

[109] To the right from the standpoint of someone on the Takamikura, facing south.

[110] Probably the double doors between where the author alighted and the Shishinden.

14
The Enthronement

His Majesty arrived, and the rite began. The Lady of the Blood[111] and I came forward to his right and left. The special assistants lifted the left and right curtain panels.[112] In his sun-jewel headdress (*tama no on-kōburi* [*benkan*]) and ceremonial robes (*raifuku*), and holding his *shaku* in perfect form, our sovereign looked thoroughly continental and gave off more than ever a radiance unknown in our realm.

Prince Proxy

Next came the Senior Nobles' salutation. The Prince Proxies[113] were Consultant Captain [Ichijō] Kimiari and, on the right, [Aburakōji] Takakage, the Intendant of the Right Watch. In their continental garb they looked foreign and very striking. The Retired Emperors' carriages stood at the South Gate.[114] Apparently their attendants wore *nōshi* or *sokutai*, as they pleased. In that broad, open space the imposingly large incense burner hardly stood out at all. Someone remarked that its smoke seemed to color the clouds above and to announce, even to China, the start of a new reign in the Land of the Rising

---

[111] *Joō*: Sukeko, an imperial granddaughter and the daughter of Sukekiyo, the head of the Office of Shrines.

[112] The role of Nako and Sukeko was purely formal. Neither actually raised a curtain panel. The relevant entry in *Yorisada ki* (quoted by Iwasa, *Zenchūshaku*, p. 52) refers to the two *tokusen* as *kamiage no jokan* and specifies that they raised curtain panels and then secured them in place (open in the shape of the character *hachi* ("eight") with needle and thread. *Sanuki-no-naishi-no-suke nikki* (also quoted by Iwasa) says on the subject, "I went through the motions of putting my hand [to the curtain]. Then the *kamiage* approached and ran needle and thread through it."

[113] *Shinnōdai*, so-called because a prince sometimes took the role of one of them. They, too, stood to left and right of the Takamikura. Normally, one was of the third rank and one of the fourth.

[114] Go-Fushimi and Hanazono may be sharing one carriage. Since a retired emperor could not attend a *sokui* rite, they are watching from the south gate of the Council of State complex.

Sun. That confirmed my conviction that our rite here matched in all ways any performed elsewhere.

kyō ya sa wa	Perhaps even Cathay
karakunibito mo	this day will come to note
kimi ga yo o	our new sovereign's reign
amatsusora yuku	by the clouds now coursing
kumo ni shiruran	across the lofty heavens.
kimi ga yo no	Our sovereign began
chiyo no hajime to	the thousand years of his reign
takamikura	on his lofty throne,
kumo no tobari o	when I raised the curtain high
kakagetsuru kana	as though sweeping back a cloud!

When it was all over we advanced as before from left and right. The special assistants lowered the curtains. HM started back, preceded by two staff women,[115] four gentlewoman assistants (*igi no nyōbō*), the four ladies-in-waiting (*myōbu*) assigned to precede him, and eight accompanying gentlewomen (*koshō*). I returned to my curtained enclosure and gave my clothes and accessories to my special assistant as a reward.[116] Those who had dressed the page girls and maids, as well as the yin-yang master who had performed the purification, were no doubt rewarded as well.

---

[115] Bearing the Sword and Jewel.

[116] That is, everything (scarlet robes and stencil-dyed train) that she had been wearing under her ritual outer garment. For her assistant, this amounted to significant income.

15
A New Era Name and a Promotion

On 4.28 the decision to change the era name came into effect. The year became Shōkyō 1. A promotion list for women officials had been announced previously.[117] Having risen to the top division (*jōkai*),[118] I rewarded Kōtō and Naishi for their help during the enthronement rite with an *unohana* fivefold set (*itsutsuginu*) and a *hitoe* in *suzushi*, cloth-wrapped and presented in a long chest (*nagabitsu*).[119] My special assistant got two robes horizontally striped in various colors and five bolts of white silk. I understood that to be the expected gift.

---

[117] On 4.11, in recognition of services performed in connection with the enthronement.

[118] Third rank and above. Since a *naishi-no-suke* normally held the fourth rank, Nako's promotion probably means that she ceased to hold that office.

[119] Presumably each woman received this gift.

16
The Kamo Festival

At Festival time I went to the palace.[120] My servants (*zōshiki*) and housemen (*saburai*) were dressed with special care. I wore:

sōbu no nioi no awase no kinu	*ao* green lined with dark plum pink
suzushi no hitoe	
kuchiba no karaginu	tan lined with yellow
kōbai no futatsu kosode	plum pink

On the Festival day itself the guards made a fine sight.[121] From the Black Door gallery His Majesty watched his envoy set out through the North Gate (*kita no jin*). The Regent was with him, as well as four or five worthy gentlewomen. The envoy, a lady, was the Shōdainagon Dame of Staff.[122]

---

120 The Kamo Festival, on the middle day of the bird in the 4th month (that year the 22nd). The author especially notes going to the palace because at her new rank she is no longer a dame of staff, hence no longer held to regular service there.
121 Officers of the Watch (*Hyōefu*) and Gate Watch (*Emonfu*), armed, with their cap tails (*ei*) rolled.
122 Fujiwara no Hideko (the future Yōrokumon-in), daughter of Sanjō Kinhide and mother of Sukō and Go-Kōgon. Go-Fushimi, Hanazono, Kōgimon-in, and Prince Yutahito watched the festival procession from stands along the way (*Hanazono-in shinki*).

17
The Emperor Visits Tokiwai House

In the 7th month His Majesty made his first progress to Tokiwai House.[123] The Retired Emperors moved to the already prepared Kogosho.[124] The idea must have been to decorate Tokiwai House particularly beautifully, so vivid were the thousand-dipped (*chishio*) purple and scarlet colors there. HM's progress was kept strictly formal since it took place by day.

The bearers set his palanquin down at the middle gate, and he alighted. A path of mats had been laid for him. He proceeded along the west gallery to the south front of the building and entered through the east double doors. That must have been the established procedure. During his three days there the former Right Minister [Imadegawa Kanesue], the Grand Counselor [Saionji Kinmune], and the Consultant Captain [probably Ōmiya Kimina] remained in attendance upon him.

---

[123] This is Kōgon's first visit as emperor to his father, Go-Fushimi. His three-day stay, unusually long, no doubt reflects satisfaction over the enthronement of a Jimyōin emperor.

[124] Kogosho ("lesser residence") seems to have meant a sort of away-from-home residence for retired emperors, since there was one at Kitayama as well.

18
The Dancing Boys

In the 8th month of that year I was on duty in the palace when Retired Emperor Go-Fushimi sent over a *chigo*[125] known as Kōwaka,[126] together with a message urging His Majesty to see him perform in some suitable setting. HM therefore summoned the boy to the customary palace court[127] and did so. The boy wore a brocade *suikan* with a pattern of dew-laden *hagi* fronds woven in high relief against a *hagi* ground. His bearing conveyed distinction and calculated elegance. The RE had had Korenari[128] teach him the dance, and he had even added to Korenari's instruction a few words of his own—hence no doubt a performance that all agreed to be flawless.

On such occasions HM's gift was a novel *suikan* or *hitatare*—with, needless to say, a fan and incense. Grand Prelate Jijū,[129] a man of fastidious taste, would collect ten boys, teach them *bugaku* dancing, dress them in delightfully fanciful costumes, and send them to the palace, where it was HM's custom to watch them. However, Kōwaka and Ato garnered praise above the rest as veritable wonders. HM also watched page boys dance, sometimes in the classic manner[130] but far more often in informal dress.

---

[125] A boy specially favored and pampered by one or more patrons. The term "catamite" comes to mind.
[126] Some have suggested that this Kōwaka may be the source, normally dated to 1393, of the medieval Kōwaka-mai drama form. See Iwasa, *Zenchūshaku*, p. 60.
[127] The *tsubo niwa* on the north side of the Seiryōden.
[128] Reizei Korenari, a close retainer of Go-Fushimi and a skilled performer on the flute.
[129] The senior monk of Yokawa and Hosshōji.
[130] With classic *bugaku* costumes and music.

19
The Flower Offering at the Chōkōdō

In the 9th month of that year I attended a flower-offering service (*kūge*) at the Chōkōdō.[131] I wore:

hagi no tate ao	*ao* green warp & *suō* weft over *ao* green
kisuji shiro suji hitoe-gasane	yellow and white horizontal stripes
kuchiba no karaginu	tan lined with yellow

The Saionji Grand Counselor [Kinmune] waited upon the Retired Emperors behind their blinds. Wine was served in the north-facing

room once they had moved there, and the Grand Counselor continued to attend them. I served them their refreshments by myself. My *kosode* was beautifully embroidered with an ivy-twined fence, just beginning to color, and, for added elegant effect, water trickling among rocks. I also wore an *ominaeshi* silk gauze (*usumono*) *hitoe*, which I slipped off my shoulders to wait on them. Saishō-no-suke[132] poured their wine.

On the way in to them there was a sliding door with a blind hung in the doorway. The blind made passage through the door so awkward that they had had it raised. However, when a gentlewoman newly arrived from Yawata[133] caught one side of her *hakama* in her mouth to hitch the garment up, the *hakama* came undone and slipped to the floor.[134] She just stood there in her heavily starched *kosode* of *suzushi*

---

[131] A *Hokke chōkō zanmai* chapel built by Retired Emperor Go-Shirakawa in the grounds of his Rokujō residence. Its generous endowment was an important Jimyōin economic asset and a bone of contention between the Jimyōin and Daikakuji imperial lines. The service mentioned was held there in the 5th and 9th months. This one was sponsored by Go-Fushimi.

[132] Presumably a senior gentlewoman attached to Go-Fushimi.

[133] Iwashimizu Hachiman. She would have been from the chief priest's family.

[134] This vignette sheds significant light on the evolution of Japanese women's clothing (Iwasa, *Zenchūshaku*, pp. 63-64). The young woman's *kosode* is her underwear. *Suzushi*

fabric, humiliatingly exposed. The two Retired Emperors roared with laughter. Looking on, I knew that I myself would have been embarrassed to death if she had not been there in any case solely for their amusement.

They drained many cups, and Saishō no Naishi-no-suke [unknown] became sufficiently tipsy to spout some distressing talk. "If only I had a presentable daughter," she said, "I would still want you to have her." It was amusing to see His Retired Majesty [Go-Fushimi] just let her chatter wash over him. Presumably things had not gone as she had hoped with her younger sister.

was semi-transparent.

20
The Moon over the Nanden

After the flower offering I was on duty in the palace while, very late one quiet night, His Majesty watched the moon in the Nanden. Not a speck of cloud roamed the clear sky, and the surface of the pond shone with exceptional brilliance. The scene was perfectly lovely. When HM retired to the back of the building,[135] the faint moonlight shining through the eaves onto the dew terrace[136] was particularly beautiful. I thought to myself:

aki fukaki	A late autumn moon
tsuyu no utena ni	casts on the dew terrace here,
kage morite	sifting through the eaves
hatsuka ni sumeru	this month's twentieth night,
nokiai no tsuki	dim yet delicate gleams.[137]

---

[135] The north aisle (*kitabisashi*).
[136] *Rodai*, a roofless, board-floored space between Shinshinden and Ninjuden.
[137] *Hatsuka* means both "dim" and "twentieth day."

21

The Purification for the Daijōsai

In the 10th month His Majesty made a progress to the purification (*gokei*).[138] The day before, the Retired Emperors had gone to the riverbank where the staff ladies rehearsed the procedure and so on. That day they went to watch the event itself.

The REs' woven-eave carriage[139] was brought up to the southern steps. The blinds in that bay were raised, Senior Nobles stood in a row, and Privy Gentlemen lined up before the carriage's shaft bench (*shiji*). Minions from their servant staff (*meshitsugi-dokoro*) attended the carriage to right and left. It started out once the yin-yang master had worked the safe-travel charm (*henbai*). The Senior RE [Go-Fushimi] wore his *nōshi* with the ankle cords tied low, and a *heirei eboshi*. This strikingly unusual way of wearing *nōshi* evoked white waves, to indescribable effect, and his own, natural radiance lent him a magnificence beyond words. His escort of twelve attendants (*mizuijin*) waited upon him seated on benches before the railing of the corner bay. In their varied costumes they looked very fine.

The Junior RE [Hanazono] left through the west double doors. His outriders' cries rang out boldly, no doubt because the Senior had lent him some of his own attendants. The Senior came to the south front, looking very impressive, and directed the carriage's approach (*kuruma yose*). Amusingly enough, the older people there chatted about reigns past, meanwhile even shedding tears. For the Junior, it was the Sanjō-bōmon Palace Minister,[140] in attendance on the east veranda, who performed the same service. Once he had boarded, the outriders advanced, uttering vigorous cries. His senior noble attendants were the Palace Minister, the Hamuro Grand Counselor Nagataka, the Reizei Former Counselor Yorisada, the Heir Apparent's Household Director Kinshige, and the Right Watch Intendant Takakage. These left their row, juniors first, to precede him. The carriages halted at Nijō-

---

[138] The purification before the Daijōsai, done beside the Kamo River; this time on 10.28.

[139] His carriage has *ajiro-bisashi,* eaves woven of bamboo or *hinoki* strips.

[140] Minamoto no Michiaki.

Madenokōji, where all sat on benches, from Senior Nobles down through gentlemen of the fourth, fifth, and sixth ranks, with attendants, so crowded together that one felt such grandeur must never have been seen before.

His Majesty's progress, too, was impressive beyond words. He stopped his palanquin for a moment before the REs' carriage and seemed to greet them. It was an extraordinary moment.

The Consort Proxy (*nyōgodai*) was an Ōinomikado.[141] That ceremony too, I gathered, was well worth seeing.

[141] On the occasion of such a purification, a woman official representing a *nyōgo* accompanied the emperor. This one was provided by Ōinomikado Fuyunobu.

22
The Kagura Rehearsals

Retired Emperor Go-Fushimi's kagura rehearsal (*hyōshi awase*) was held on 11.4.[142]

The kagura musicians were:

Rhythm (*hyōshi*) and	Lord of Civil Affairs [Nakamikado] Fuyusada
	Acting Counselor [Tōin] Sanemori[143]
Voice	Heir Apparent's Deputy Household Director Munekane
	Left Captain [Nijō] Sukekane
	[Ayanokōji] Atsuari
Wagon	Acting Grand Counselor [Ōinomikado] Fuyunobu
Fue	Left Captain [Reizei] Korenari
Hichiriki	Former Right Gate Watch Intendant [Yamamomo] Kanetaka

Pieces played in the concert (*asobi*) afterwards:

In *ryo* mode:
Ana tōto
Torinoha
Mushiroda
Tori no kyū
Mimasaka
Katen no kyū

In *ritsu* mode:
Ise no umi
Manzairaku
Koromogae
Sandai no kyū

Rhythm	Acting Counselor Sanemori
Voice	Munekane
Shō	Left Captain Takatsune
Biwa	Retired Emperor [Go-Fushimi]
	Former Right Minister Kikutei-dono [Imadegawa Kanetaka]
Sō-no-koto	[Nakamikado] Fuyusada

---

[142] Rehearsal for the kagura and concert (*asobi*) to be held in the Seishodō.
[143] A younger brother of Tōin Kinkata, the author of *Entairyaku*.

The Junior RE held his rehearsal on the 7th.

The kagura musicians were:

Rhythm and Voice	Acting Counselor Sanemori
	Munekane
	[Hachijō] Kiyosue
	Atsuari
	Sukekane
	The lower official (*jige*) Tadaari
Wagon	Fuyunobu
Fue	Korenari
Hichiriki	Kanetaka

And for the concert:

In *ryo* mode:

Ana tōto

Torinoha

Mushiroda

Tori no kyū

In *ritsu* mode:

Ise no umi

Manzairaku

Rōei (*Reigetsu* and *Tokuze*)

Kanshū

Rhythm	Sanemori
Voice	Munekane
Shō	Left Captain Naritsune
Biwa	Counselor Sanetada
Sō-no-koto	Fuyusada

Otherwise, as for the kagura.

23
The Gosechi Dancers

On the 11th, His Majesty made a progress to the Council of State Office,[144] where he settled into the North Pavilion (*kōbō*) and the Morning Pavilion (*aitandokoro*). The gentlewoman's quarters (*tsubone*) were next to the *tsukuriai*.[145] These five presented Gosechi dancers:[146] the Kasanoin Acting Counselor Nagasada, Lord Saionji [Kinmune], the Hino Grand Counselor [Sukena], and the Acting Counselor [Toshizane]. The dancer formally selected (*mairi*) came from Lord Saionji.[147] These silks spilled out (*uchiide*) under the blinds:

white robes	white
white *hitoe*	white
suō no uwagi	maroon
moegi no karaginu	grass green

The *uwagi* bore an exceptionally well done, woven relief pattern of beautifully colored combs,[148] and the white waves on the sleeves could have been breaking on Sode-no-ura.[149] The other dancers wore the usual colors. None stood out particularly.

On the 11th[150] HM repaired to the curtained dais (*chōdai*).[151] He wore *sashinuki*[152] tied low at the ankles (*ge-kukuri*), with the skirts spilling through. The dancers mounted the stage (*dai ni noboru*). HM watched them. The privy gentlemen sang "Bintatara"[153] in the northern gallery. He returned as dawn was beginning to lighten the clouds. The two head chamberlains, Munekane and Yorinori, accompanied him.

On 12th there was a drinking party in the privy chamber (*tenjō no ensui*). The Head Chamberlains and the others wore *nōshi* with *uchiki* in

---

[144] In the old place grounds.
[145] Perhaps the place where a *watadono* gallery linked the Kōbō to the Aitandokoro.
[146] Actually, only four.
[147] According to *Hanazono-in shinki* the others were offered "privately" (*missan*).
[148] A comb pattern is special to the Gosechi event.
[149] "Sleeve Shore," an *utamakura* in Dewa.
[150] The evening of the dancers' arrival.
[151] In the Jōneiden to see the dance rehearsal, according to custom.
[152] As he never did otherwise.
[153] As always on this occasion.

various colors, and all let their skirts spill through. At the third cup they bared a shoulder and boisterously danced *Manzairaku*. HM watched in imperial dress, seated in his chair *(isu)* by the Privy Chamber *(kami no to)*.[154] The Saionji Grand Counselor awaited HM's pleasure to the left of the double doors. Many gentlewomen surrounded his chair, with their skirts over their heads.

On the 13th they brought in the mark posts.[155] The two Controllers responsible, and the Governors[156] and their juniors were present. They came in through the Suzaku Gate[157] and proceeded through the south gate of the Council of State headquarters into the southern court.

The dancers took their places in the Presence for the rehearsal. The page girls and maids did not enter the gallery. The best singers among the Privy Gentlemen were summoned into the Presence and sang all their songs. As on the 12th, there was a drinking party in the Privy Chamber.

The Senior Nobles waited upon HM for the page-girl viewing.[158] The page girls approached along the gallery and presented themselves on the veranda. The Privy Gentlemen followed them with tapers *(shisoku)*.[159] The maids presented themselves outside on the ground, assisted by sixth-rankers. A cold wind was blowing, and the pearly hailstones falling on their sleeves looked very pretty.

karatama no	Jewels they might be,
kazashi to miete	bringing from beyond the sea
otomego ga	new gleams of beauty,
tachimau sode ni	the hailstones now falling
furu arare kana	on the girls' dancing sleeves.

HM proceeded to the Kairyūden, where he bathed.[160] He wore a white silk *hō*. Those attending him wore *omigoromo*. He returned at

---

[154] Not the palace privy chamber, but a room assimilated to it.

[155] *Hyō no ki*, the decorated indicators placed to show where the Sukiden and Yukiden (the twin Daijōsai pavilions) were to be erected.

[156] Of Ōmi and Tanba, which provided the materials for the Sukiden and Yukiden.

[157] The south gate into the greater palace compound *(daidairi)*.

[158] The page girls and maids in attendance on the Gosechi dancers were called before the emperor for his inspection.

[159] Slender pine torches for use indoors.

dawn. It was raining, and everyone got very wet. The Regent's[161] ceremonial train (*shita-gasane*) was all but ruined. The way Lady Sanmi mourned privately that some impediment must stand between him and playing his part in the day's rites was quite amusing. Nonetheless he swiftly did so, looking splendid.

Ceremonial train

[160] This purification precedes his offerings and his encounter with the gods in the Yukiden and Sukiden. The expression *kairyūden gyōgō* (progress to the Kairyūden) alone evokes unambiguously the Daijōsai rite that follows.
[161] Takatsukasa Fuyunori. Lady Sanmi, below, is probably his wife.

24
The Gosechi Festival and the Toyo-no-akari

The festival began on the 14th.
On the 15th there were kagura and a concert in the Seishodō.[162]

Rhythm	Acting Counselor Sukechika
and	Acting Counselor Sanemori
Voice	Munekane
	Sukeyo
	Kiyosue
	Sukekane
	Atsuari, and others
Wagon	Acting Grand Counselor Fuyunobu
Fue	Korenari
Hichiriki	Former Right Gate Watch Intendant Kanetaka

Pieces performed in the concert afterwards:

in *ryo* mode:
> *Ana tōto*
> *Torinoha*
> *Minoyama*
> *Katen no kyū*

In *ritsu* mode:
> *Ise no umi*
> *Manzairaku*
> *Gojōraku*

Rhythm	Acting Counselor Sanemori
Voice	Munekane
	Atsuari
Shō	The Right Minister [Ōmiya Suehira] (playing Kangie)[163]
Fue	Korenari
Biwa	The Chancellor [Imadegawa Kanesue]
Sō-no-koto	Fuyusada
Wagon	Acting Grand Counselor Fuyunobu

---

[162] A part of the Burakuin. After the loss of the Burakuin, the event was held in the gallery of the Kōbō, a part of the Council of State office complex.
[163] A famous *shō*. There were actually two, a greater and a smaller.

HM sat on his dais at the *tsukuriai*. The performers took their seats at his command. That night the Chancellor [Kanesue] was also to present formal thanks for his appointment.

HM looked into each Gosechi dancers' dressing room. In ours he was delighted to note accessory boxes (*uchimidare no hako*), lined with thin paper and filled with combs, hidden under a two-tiered cabinet (*nikai*). A strict prohibition had prevented any exchange of combs, and this had so disappointed my father that he put them there secretly.[164]

From the Saionji Grand Counselor [Kinmune], incense arrived in a gold fish-case (*gyotai no hako*) attached to an artificial pine branch. (The case came in an accessory box lined with thin paper.) Kasanoin [Nagasada] sent comb-shaped aloeswood (*jinkō*) and musk (*jakō*) incense to Tokiwai House. My house was informed that Kitayama, too,[165] wished a particular person to have Gosechi incense, which I therefore presented as requested. I put it in a gold box decorated with a pattern of linked combs, which I laid in an accessory box lined with thin, scarlet paper bearing colored words from *Minoyama*.[166] On the days when the Privy Gentlemen came round to Tokiwai House, they kept roaming back and forth all night and into dawn, until I was completely exhausted.[167]

HM had the mark posts brought to the Kōbō and viewed them.

One night HM went to the Seishodō. Not a speck of cloud roamed a limit sky, and the ground within the palace walls stretched away[168] under bright moonlight that, here, had a quality beyond words. From within a fence surrounded by guards there issued so foul a stench that he hastily returned whence he had come. What a shame!

On the 16th came the Toyo-no-akari festivity.[169] HM mounted the Takamikura, and the dancers entered his presence. The Privy

---

[164] A prohibition forbade excessively luxurious display. Elaborate combs, a Gosechi tradition, were exchanged as gifts.

[165] Eifukumon-in, who lived at Kitayama.

[166] A *saibara* that celebrates the delights of Toyo-no-akari.

[167] After the Gosechi drinking party, the privy gentlemen and others visited the residence of the retired emperor and other such places, boisterously singing and dancing.

[168] At the time, little stood within these walls. The grounds were vacant, apart from a few Council of State buildings.

Gentlemen twice danced "Bintatara" boisterously in the gallery (*nobori rō*).[170] As the hours wore on, frost glittered under a brilliant moon that seemed to gather all the beauty of the night.

fukuru yo no	In the depths of night,
kumo no kayoiji	clouds roaming the heavens
shimo saete	distill winter rime,
otome no sode ni	until frozen moonlight
kooru tsukikage	glitters on the dancers' sleeves.

---

[169] The emperor partakes of the first fruits in the Shinshinden (the Council of State headquarters), then enjoys a drinking feast with his officials.
[170] The gallery between the Council of State building proper and the Kōbō.

25
A Night with Kinmune

To my surprise I had found myself spending nights away from home when, early in the second month,[171] I awoke in the usual house to the singing of birds and the sound of bells. They brought up my carriage under a misty dawn sky. The clouds resting on the hilltops were just beginning to brighten, and from somewhere the wandering breeze brought the fragrance of plum blossoms. It was all perfectly lovely, and although I was still too dull at the time really to appreciate it, it is present to me even now.

They drew my carriage up to the monks' lodge at Tokiwai House.[172] I alighted and went to lie down. That morning Shōshō[173] came to let me know that [the Retired Emperor] wanted me. She teased me when she saw that I had only just slipped out of my nightclothes (*yoru no koromo*). Having no answer, I lay there with the bedding (*tonoimono*) over my head, and she jokingly tried to pull it off me. The happy memory feels like only yesterday.

---

[171] Of the same year as the Daijōsai (Shōkyō 1.11), but months earlier, still in Genkō 2 (1332). (Shōkyō started only on 4.28.) She and Kinmune are sleeping together not at his house or hers, but at a place associated with Tokiwai House, the residence of Retired Emperors Go-Fushimi and Hanazono.

[172] For the sake of discretion. Nako goes to lie down in her *tsubone*, her room in Tokiwai House as a gentlewomen to Go-Fushimi.

[173] A gentlewoman attached to Go-Fushimi.

26
Marriage

On the first day of spring, that year when I lived at home,[174] he sent me on thin, scarlet paper, beautifully perfumed:

aratama no	At last it is here,
toshi machiete mo	the New Year, long awaited,
itsushika to	and I now foresee
kimi ni zo chigiru	spending in your company
yukusue no haru	many future springs.

I answered on paper of the same color:

yukusue no	Your future company
chigiri mo shiranu	remains a mystery to me,
nagame ni wa	nor can I foresee
aratamaruran	what new spring might yet come
haru mo shirarezu	to dispel my sadness.

It was agreed now that, in the absence of any decisive impediment, I would receive him at home (*machi-miru*). My future seemed to have been settled all too abruptly, and I felt somehow anxious and sad.

---

[174] Shōkyō 2.1.13 (1333). She is no longer in court service.

27
Last Service at the Palace

Spring came on 1.12.[175] His Majesty was to move to another pavilion because of the directional taboo,[176] and he asked repeatedly for me to come to him, however briefly. I made up my mind to go. Some tried to persuade me not to,[177] but I went anyway. I wore a fivefold set in a *tsubomi kōbai* layering. The new Dame of Staff[178] had gone to the Ninjuden to receive the Sword. The gentlewomen wore fivefold sets. The refreshment boxes (*warigo*) provided by Lord Kitayama [Kinmune] arrived with it. Lady Sanmi[179] served the meal, then took my place. I remained in attendance for a while, but there were embarrassing remarks, and I slipped out.[180] After the wine he [Kinmune] withdrew, and I attended HM, who was toying with a fan. He showed me the ornaments (*okimono*) that had adorned the meal. *Miyako wa nobe* was just as pretty as it could be.[181]

I withdrew at dawn and started toward my carriage, which awaited me at the long bridge (*nagahashi*). The brightening sky, with clouds trailing over the hills, was quite lovely. I promised everyone seeing me off that I would be back on about the 20th. Alas, I would never see the palace again.

On the 12th [Kōgimon-in] made her formal entrance into the palace (*judai*). She wore:

yanagi sakura	lightest pink lined with lightest purple
kurenai no hitoe	scarlet

---

[175] *Setsubun*, the day before the previous entry.

[176] The emperor normally moved elsewhere for the night of *setsubun* and returned after the bell announcing dawn. Apparently Kōgon moved from the Seiryōden to the Ninjuden.

[177] Her marriage to Kinmune is to be acknowledged the next day.

[178] Nako's replacement, probably the Fujiwara no Hideko of no. 16.

[179] Perhaps Nako's grandmother Hiroko, the wife of Hino Toshimitsu. At any rate, she is not the same as the Lady Sanmi mentioned in no. 23.

[180] *Suberi-idenu* refers also to the way she moved, on her knees and shins.

[181] Apparently some sort of ornament, accessory, or set of the same, evoking *Kokinshū* 19: *Miyama niwa/ matsu wa yuki dani/ kienaku ni/ miyako wa nobe no/ wakana tsumikeri* (In the hills, snow still lies on the pines, but in the meadows of the capital we have picked spring shoots).

kōbai no uwagi	plum pink
ebizome no kouchiki	grape purple
aoiro no karaginu	*ao* green
suzushi no hakama	

Rō-no-onkata[182] accompanied her in her carriage, wearing an *ume* layering. The Prince[183] apparently shared the carriage, too.

The Blue Roans festival (*aouma no sechie*) began at noon. Kōtō and Shōshō put up my hair (*kamiage*).[184] I had eight gentlewoman assistants (*igi no nyōbō*). The event on the 16th was approaching fast.[185]

---

[182] A gentlewoman attached to Kōgimon-in.

[183] Prince Yutahito, Kōgimon-in's son and the future Emperor Kōmyō, in his thirteenth year.

[184] Built up high over the forehead, as customarily under formal circumstances.

[185] The *Onna tōka no sechie* took place on the 16th. The emperor watched women dance and sing in the court before the Shinshinden and offered a banquet afterwards. The conflict about to break out forced the cancellation of this one.

28
Meetings During the Turmoil

On the 20th I was to be on duty in the palace, but the difficulties that arose forced a postponement. Word came that morning that the world was in turmoil, and the Grand Counselor [Kinmune] went to wait upon the Retired Emperor [Go-Fushimi]. He was not alone. I hurried there as well. Guards surrounded the gate of Tokiwai House so strictly that a carriage could hardly get in, nor was it possible in practice for carriages taking gentlewomen to attend the RE either to enter or to leave the grounds; still less could one get through on the way to a private assignation.[186] However, calm soon returned, and for two or three days we managed to steal away to be together.

One morning, after a night when he had failed to come because, [his letter said] "There are still those who oppose my leaving, and in any case a particular difficulty keeps me from you," he sent me this:

ika ni sen	O what could I do
itsuwari naranu	were you to deem after all
itsuwari o	a fib what was not one
nao itsuwari to	and, despite everything,
omoinasareba	insist that I told a lie?

This was because on a past occasion he had sent me:

itsuwari no	Which one of us, then,
ta ga narawashi zo	leans toward telling lies?
hitorine wa	Sleeping all alone?
sashi mo yona yona	No, I just cannot believe
sareji to omou ni	that is your way every night.[187]

A measure of peace had returned, and I was living at home when one day I went [to Tokiwai House]. Some urged me not to for another few days, but the RE was asking for me so I went nonetheless, without

---

[186] She refers to seeing Kinmune.
[187] Kinmune seems in this poem to suspect Nako, presumably unfairly, of having another lover. Could he have Go-Fushimi in mind?

a word to Kinmune. He then came to see me and found out where I had gone.

The next morning:

sate mo nao	Why, so be it, then.
chigirishi sue no	But if we two, together,
kawarazu wa	still have a future,
asu no yuube ya	we might after all agree
tanomi narubeki	to count on tomorrow night.

I answered:

sadame naki	Like all the others,
kinoo no kure no	the evening yesterday
narai ni wa	slipped through our hands,
asu no chigiri mo	and now I see little hope
ikaga tanoman	of meeting you tomorrow.

29
Before the Storm

That spring there had been [at Tokiwai House] a competition list (*kakitsuke*) pairing people to gather pine seedlings on the day of the rat, tie them to plum boughs, and offer them to Kannon.[188] One night I slipped away on my usual errand[189] without realizing that list members and partners had been decided. I heard about it only when I returned the next morning. "Why, I must not have been listed!" I remarked to someone nearby. The Retired Emperor heard me. "They were looking for you last night," he said, "but apparently you were away. I can hardly imagine that you were actually left off it."

I was so embarrassed that I hardly knew what to do with myself. "I have brought *ushi-hitsuji* gifts from Lord Kitayama," I said.[190] With me I had, in a gold willow box,[191] a deep lapis-lazuli blue jar accompanied by a pair of *uchieda*—peach and azalea—and a letter.[192] I placed the box before the RE, and an attendant presented it for his inspection, together (I believe) with some wine. The RE told me to write the reply, since he had no one else suitable waiting on him. At the time I was feeling far too awkward to take up the brush, so I murmured an excuse and slipped out. It is amusing to remember now how guilty I felt.

---

[188] Apparently a flashback to the first month of Shōkyō 2 (1333). The festive game in question seems to have paired participants one against the other in an elaboration on the venerable custom of pulling up seedling pines (emblems of longevity and good fortune) on the month's first day of the rat. It probably also involved making poems.

[189] To meet Kinmune.

[190] The year of Go-Fushimi's birth suggests that this *ushi-hitsuji* day (1.18 in Shōkyō 2) was ill-omened for him (*suibi*) according to yin-yang lore and therefore called for a gift.

[191] *Yanaibako*, a lidded box properly made of slender slips of willow wood, cut three-sided and sewn together with thread. This one apparently mimics a *yanaibako* in gold.

[192] An *uchieda* (or *uchioki*) is an artificial, silver or gold flower placed on a *kosode* to keep it in place when carried in an open box (*hirobuta*).

Early in the intercalary 2nd month I was unwell and went home. The illness was not serious, but it dragged on, and I received those who came to see me lying down. The 20th was past when I felt better and went to Tokiwai House. People there remarked that I was still not myself. "What could be the matter be?" the Junior RE [Hanazono] said. "This is very strange. I wonder about your pulse. Let me examine it for you." "I really have no idea," I answered. "This is just an aftereffect of my illness." I moved to leave, but he took my pulse anyway and advised me on how to look after myself. It was a curious moment. Being versed in yin-yang lore as well as in physic, he also sought an answer from divination. That was curious, too.

30

The Reigning and Retired Emperors Move to Rokuhara

On the 3.16[193] His Majesty and the Retired Emperors, Senior and Junior, repaired to Rokuhara.[194] Neither I nor anyone else had the least idea what to do, so I will write no more on that. Anything I might say would probably be wrong. The gentlewomen could not possibly attend them, but they also could not leave them unattended, so a few joined them after all. I hardly saw how I could go myself, and people[195] sought to dissuade me from trying, reminding me what a miserable figure I would cut under such dreadful circumstances; so I decided to look in only briefly and went there with Lady Nii.[196]

Screens stood between Their Majesties, and the small space was full of people. The REs wore *nōshi* because HM was present. The Heir Apparent, in his fourteenth or fifteenth year, was still dressed as a boy (*warawa sugata*).[197] He occupied the middle gate gallery (*chūmon watadono*). Savage (*ebisu*) forms[198] were visible very close. It felt like an unknown world.

I had expected to remain on duty that night and later, but word came that an attack[199] was expected at dawn. Warrior authority (*buke*) ordered the gentlewomen to leave, so each tidied up and called for her carriage to go home. It was not at all what I had in mind. The gentle-women's room (*oyudono no ue*) and that of the servants (*suezama*) were divided only by screens, and men and women mingled there in a most unseemly way. Armed savages crowded close, urging any carriage on its way out to leave as quickly as possible. Eight women rode off in mine. At the main gate we encountered Lady Sanjō's[200] The backs of

---

[193] Actually, the 12th.

[194] The previous day Akamatsu Norimura had defeated the Rokuhara forces and burst into Kyoto. The imperial persons sought refuge in the Rokuhara north compound, in the pavilion belonging to Hōjō Nakatoki.

[195] Probably her father and her women.

[196] Ujiko, the wife of Saionji Sanehira.

[197] Prince Yasuhito, a grandson of Go-Nijō, had not yet come of age.

[198] Warriors in armor.

[199] By Akamatsu forces.

[200] Hideko, daughter of Sanjō Kinhide.

both carriages were therefore brought together, and four of them moved to hers. The Junior RE's Lady Sanmi[201] said, "Never mind what happens to me. I simply cannot leave him." She stayed behind, alone. Everyone wondered in despair what the world was coming to. Meanwhile, it was night by the time we reached Lady Nii's residence.[202] There we parted, each—Kōtō, Shinhyōe, and I—to go to her own home.

---

[201] Saneko, daughter of Ōgimachi Saneaki. A favorite of Hanazono, three years later she had a son formally attributed to him but actually Kōgon's.
[202] The Saionji establishment at Ichijō-Imadegawa.

31
Parting at Kiyomizu

Dawn came, but that day nothing happened.[203] Kiyokage brought a letter from Rokuhara. It said, "I had hoped that we might at least meet somewhere else, but the confusion was too great. It is so frustrating!" and so on. He [Kinmune] described what was happening. Kiyokage wore a particularly showy, light orange (*kō*) *hitatare* over what they apparently call arm guards (*kote*). The silver fittings showed through the sleeves, which could easily have been distasteful, had his behavior not been so at all. On the contrary, he seemed to have acquired a dignity above his normal station.

Their Majesties stay at Rokuhara was indescribably burdensome. My father,[204] who had to remain with them, moved to lodgings near Kiyomizu. [Kinmune] must have feared that his absence would weigh on me more and more, because he sent a message urging me to move there as well; so I suddenly ended up doing so.

The 20th of the 4th month passed, every day meanwhile threatening disaster. One evening [Kinmune] turned up there, saying that he had seized an opportunity to get away. All too soon birds were singing and bells booming hither and yon. "I must be hearing things," he said, brushing it off; but his people reminded him repeatedly that it would not look right if he were still there when dawn came. They opened the double doors. The dawn moon was very bright, and the *hagi* near the eaves was taller than usual at this season. Light gleamed from the dew on every leaf, even the lowest, until the lightening sky seemed to belong less to summer than to autumn. The scene would have been moving enough at any time, but now, amid such turmoil that one feared there might be no tomorrow, both his leaving and my staying aroused only misery.

---

[203] The Akamatsu forces fought those of Rokuhara in the vicinity of Yamazaki and Iwashimizu Hachiman, but in the capital there was indeed a lull. The Kiyokage about to be mentioned is a Saionji houseman.

[204] Just as Nako never writes Kinmune's name, she also avoids the word for "father." Here, Sukena is *waga tanomu hito*, "the one upon whom I rely." Sukena is the retired emperors' chief administrator (*shikken*).

Dawn was coming on. He called for his comb and set off. I left the room open and remained lying there, gazing outside. Suddenly the sky clouded over and the last, lingering moonlight vanished. For some reason this poem came to me:

ika ni sen	What am I to do
omokage shitau	when that beloved figure,
ariake no	under a dawn moon
tsuki sae kumoru	hidden now behind the clouds,
kinuginu no sora	leaves me under a blank sky?

32
The Sweet-flag Root

All had heaved a sigh of relief upon learning that the eastern savages were on their way, and the incomprehensible news that they had turned their bows elsewhere was deeply upsetting.[205] On 5.5 all hope seemed gone, and I was in dark despair when this arrived from him, on white *usuyō* paper:

numamizu ni	This long sweet-flag root
ouru ayame no	growing in marshy waters
nagaki ne mo	I drew out in sign
kimi ga chigiri no	of the bond between us two
tameshi ni zo hiku	for many long years to come.
kakenareshi	This root is the same
sode no ukine wa	on my sleeve, and the same, too,
kawaranedo	the bitter tears I weep;
nani no ayame mo	yet, today, nothing else
wakanu kyō kana	makes any sense at all.

and at the very end:

wasurezu wa	For as long, I beg,
katami to mo miyo	as I linger in your thoughts,
aware kono	remember me by this;
kyō shi mo nokosu	today I leave you, alas,
miziguki no ato	only traces of my brush.

The box lid, lined with scarlet and purple-dyed *usuyō*, contained a *kusudama*.[206]

---

[205] Turned their bows against the men of Kamakura. On 4.16 Nagoe Takaie and Ashikaga Takauji left Kamakura. On the 27th Takaie died in battle at Koganawate, and that day, at Shinomura Hachiman Takauji raised troops to defeat the Hōjō.
[206] Attached to a sweet flag (*ayame*) root: a fifth-month gift. A *kusudama* is a purificatory ball of incense wrapped in brocade, decorated with artificial flowers and trailing five-colored threads.

I answered:

asaki e ni	This sweet-flag root drawn,
hiku ya ayame no	I gather, from shallow waters:
ukine o mo	am I to hold it
nagaki tameshi to	forever here on my sleeve
ware ya kakubeki	in hope of long years to come?
nokoshi oku	In your memory,
katami to kikeba	you say, you leave me these:
miru kara ni	traces of your brush
ne nomi nakaruru	that I cannot bear to see
mizuguki no ato	without shedding anguished tears.

33
Defeat

On the 7th of the month they surrounded Rokuhara and attacked it from all directions. This was no surprise, but all were horrified nonetheless when it actually happened. That night they set fire to Rokuhara.

I pictured Their Majesties engulfed by smoke, sure that I must be dreaming. But had they really escaped the flames? I lay sleepless all night, my thoughts upon them, my spirit gone from my body. News that they had set out eastward was not at all reassuring, since that direction was far from safe. In black despair, I wondered what news of them would reach me next.[207]

Attitudes had suddenly changed, and it was just as well to be cautious. I stole away from where I had been staying, went first to that chapel,[208] and then, on the 9th, found myself at home. That was dangerous, too, though. I secretly moved instead to Agui, where I had a connection.[209]

On the 10th, one of his gentlewomen apparently found out, through someone she knew there, where I was. She told me that he had gone with Their Majesties, but that, to his dismay, his people had somehow conspired to part him from them. I was distraught, not to know what had become of them. She was glad to have found me, and a carriage came immediately. I doubted the wisdom of wandering off like that and had no wish to move, but I weakly gave in when everyone else urged me to go. They brought the carriage up to the Myōon-dō,[210] where I alighted. I had thought to be there only briefly, but days went by, and I felt completely lost.

---

[207] *Baishōron* ("Takauji Attacks Rokuhara") describes their flight.

[208] *Midō*, unidentified.

[209] The person she knows may be Shiba no Zenni, her father's second wife. Agui (the customary reading is a contraction of "Angoin"), a city temple attached to Chikurin-in on Mount Hiei, was the headquarters of a line of popular preachers.

[210] A temple or chapel on the Saionji Kitayama estate, dedicated to Myōon Tennyo, the divine patron of the biwa.

34
The Imperial Persons Return to Kyoto
Kinmune's Despair

The unspeakable news reached me that one Gonomiya[211] had lodged Their Majesties somewhere called Ibuki, in Ōmi. Then came a request from the current Shogun [Takauji] for a messenger to accompany the imperial chest [containing the regalia] to Ibuki. A [Saionji] houseman was therefore dispatched. My husband informed me that Ujimitsu,[212] who had been leading the Retired Emperor's mount, had been struck by a stray arrow and had remained behind. He had made the effort to go to see him. I added to my reply:

kakute dani	I who, as things stand,
sutenu narai no	still cannot reject the world
mi no usa wa	suffer misery
omoishi yori mo	beyond my imagining.
ararekeru kana	Yet, for all that, he still lives!

On 5.27 Their Majesties returned to the capital.[213] The news that my father and brother had returned in mossy robes was a fresh shock.[214]

Under these dreadful circumstances I asked to return home, but he forbade even a brief visit. There were people I longed to write to, but he feared such serious consequences, should any such letter go astray, that I gave up even that. Instead I remained miserably confined, most unwillingly compelled to follow a course that I was afraid others might condemn, and my distress was all the greater.

Meanwhile, he remained so absorbed in the unexpected misery of having failed to continue on with Their Majesties that he talked of nothing but disturbing subjects like wishing to renounce the world. "Could I really simply cut you adrift, though?" he would say, "after so insisting that you must be my wife?" It was sad that he should worry

---

[211] Go-Daigo's fifth son. According to *Masukagami*, he led the Southern Court forces that annihilated Rokuhara at Banba.
[212] Her younger brother.
[213] Kōgon, too, is now a retired emperor. The three entered Jimyōin House on the 28th.
[214] Sukena and Nako's elder brother Fusamitsu have renounced the world.

that way even about *me*, who, after all, hardly matter. He appeared so intent on renunciation that, despite Their Jimyōin Majesties' repeated attempts to dissuade him, I could not help wondering what lay ahead. Perhaps the views of people whose opinion he respected prevailed in the end, though, because he came after all to take a somewhat more reassuring view of the matter.

35
Nako Moves to Kitayama

The middle of the 6th month came. I suppose it was the prospect of having my hitherto clandestine existence recognized that made me hesitate to visit my family immediately, and I was very happy when he nonetheless granted me a brief stay. When I reached the city, though, nothing I saw or heard was what it had been before, and I felt sadder than ever.

Two or three days later a carriage came for me and took me back. I wondered on the way what lay ahead, and in countless ways I felt agonizingly insecure.

I have run on so far about matters that could not possibly interest anyone else, and I might say a good deal more; but not now.

THE DEATH OF KINMUNE
AND THE BIRTH OF NAKO'S SON

From *TAIHEIKI* 13
"Kitayama no muhon no koto"

At the time of the battle for Kamakura during Genkō [1331-1334], the novice Shirō Sakon no Tayū [Hōjō Yasuie], younger brother to the late Sagami Novice [Hōjō Takatoki], pretended to kill himself and secretly fled the town. He spent some time in Mutsu and then, to avoid being recognized, returned to lay life and went up to Kyoto.

There he approached the Saionji establishment, where he remained in the guise of a provincial warrior serving his first lord. He did so because during the Jōkyū conflict, secret intelligence sent to the Kanto by the Chancellor, Lord Saionji Kintsune, had that day given Hōjō Yoshitoki victory in battle; and for that reason Yoshitoki, on his deathbed, had enjoined his descendants for seven generations to trust the Saionji house. The Hōjō therefore remained forever grateful to the Saionji.

So it was that most Empresses, reign after reign, were Saionji daughters, and over half the appointees to provincial office were Saionji. So it was, too, that every Saionji head became Chancellor and reached the very highest rank. No doubt it was the Kanto's [the Hōjō's] enduring gratitude toward the Saionji that moved the late Takatoki to aspire to restore the fortunes of his house and regain government over the realm, personally control the court, and hold in his grasp the four seas. With that ambition in mind he had Yasuie return to lay life, change his name to Gyōbu no Shō Tokioki, and devote his every thought, day and night, to rebellion.

One night the chief Saionji administrator [Miyoshi Bunhira] came before the Grand Counselor [Kinmune] and said, "Nothing better reveals whether a realm is rising or falling than the manner, good or bad, in which it is governed; and this manner is best judged by considering whether it employs or dismisses wise officials. Thus Yin fell once Wei Zi had left it, and condemning Fan Zen finished the King of Chu. The only wise nobleman at present is Fujifusa, who foresaw disaster and withdrew from the world: a great loss for the court and great good fortune for your house.[215] If you are prepared to act decisively, one hundred thousand of those who served your forebears will flock to you and overthrow the current regime within a day." Such was his advice.

Lord Kinmune took it. He appointed Tokioki commander in Kyoto and mobilized men from the Kinai and the neighboring provinces. He appointed Tokioki's nephew, Sagami no Jirō Tokiyuki, commander in the Kanto and gave him the men of Kai, Shinano, Musashi, and Sagami. He named Nagoya no Tarō Tokikane commander in the north and assembled troops from Etchū, Noto, and Kaga. Then he specified the signal that would call each body of men to battle.

That done, he summoned carpenters from the west of the capital and had them build, from nothing, a new bathhouse: one so designed that whoever trod upon a section of its access walk would fall onto upright steel blades. The Emperor [Go-Daigo] was to set out on an excursion and accept an invitation to a bathhouse party like those at the Huaqing Palace hot spring.[216] He would then fall into the trap. Once all was ready and the warriors were in place, Lord Kinmune invited the Emperor to Kitayama to view the autumn leaves. The day was set, and the excursion protocol was arranged.

It had been announced that the imperial excursion was to take place at the hour of the horse [noon] the next day when, that night, the Emperor dropped off to sleep and had a dream. A woman wearing two grey robes over a red *hakama* came to him. "Raging tigers and wolves are before you," she said, "and behind you are savage bears. You must cancel your excursion tomorrow." "Where are you from?" the dream-

---

[215] Madenokōji Fujifusa (1296-1380?), an important Go-Daigo supporter, played a major official role in the Kenmu Restoration before renouncing the world in 1334.

[216] The Tang emperor Taizong's palace at Lishan, where he disported himself with Yang Guifei. This would not have been Go-Daigo's first visit to Kitayama. He had previously gone there at least in 1319 and 1331 to visit his empress, the youngest daughter of Saionji Sanekane. In 1331 Kinmune, already the head of the Saionji house, was his host. At Kitayama, during Go-Daigo's exile, Kinmune also saw to the care of his sons by a certain Naishi-no-sanmi, who had accompanied him to Oki (Perkins, *The Clear Mirror*, pp. 164, 186-187, 205). According to *Baishōron* ("Warriors and Courtiers: Fire and Water"), during Kenmu Go-Daigo "made several sudden, apparently casual visits to Kitayama on days when fighting [between him and Takauji] threatened to break out, in order to keep those who mattered there informed."

ing Emperor asked. "I have long inhabited the Shinsen-en,"[217] his visitor replied and went away. The Emperor then awoke.

"What a horrid dream!" he thought to himself. Still, the excursion was all arranged, and he could hardly imagine canceling it at the last minute. Already he was being invited to board the imperial palanquin. Nonetheless, the dream had so troubled him that he proceeded first to the Shinsen-en and made an offering there to the dragon god. The water in the garden lake suddenly changed. No wind blew, yet white waves beat upon the shore. Increasingly disturbed by the dream's warning, he stopped his palanquin to give the matter further thought.

Just then the Chikurin-in Counselor Kinshige[218] came galloping up. "The Saionji Grand Counselor Kinmune has proposed this excursion in order to further a secret plot of his devising," he said. "So I have just been informed. You must return to your residence immediately, summon Suetsune, Haruhira, and Bunhira, and question them."

The Emperor gathered from the dream warning the previous night, and from the way the lake water had suddenly changed, that there was indeed reason to take the matter seriously. He went straight home; called in the Nakanoin Captain Sadahira, the Yūki Magistrate Chikamitsu, and Nagatoshi, the Governor of Hōki; and ordered them to bring him Kinmune, Toshisue, and Bunhira.

Promptly, over two thousand mounted men divided into forces for the main gate and the back, and surrounded the Kitayama residence on all sides, seven or eight deep. Kinmune saw immediately that his plot had been discovered, but he nonetheless betrayed no dismay. His wife, the gentlewomen, and the retainers, who knew nothing of the affair, cried out in alarm and fled or collapsed in utter confusion. At the sight of the imperial force his younger brother, the quick-witted Toshisue, slipped out alone and, from the hill behind the compound, fled wherever his steps might take him.

Sadahira calmly explained to Kinmune what had brought things to this pass. Kinmune replied, almost in tears, "Incompetent though I am,

---

[217] The emperor's private, walled garden. The "visitor" is probably Seiryū Gongen, properly the protector deity of Daigoji, who manifested herself in the Shinsen-en in answer to prayers for rain addressed to the dragon gods by Kūkai.
[218] Kinmune's younger half brother.

I have the late Empress's good will to thank for offices and emoluments that have allowed me nonetheless to hold my head up in the world.[219] In truth, I owe them entirely to my sovereign's enlightened compassion. How, then, could I possibly wish from the shadows to break the branch that supports me or to muddy the spring from which I drink? I can only imagine that since my house has for generations enjoyed honor and prosperity beyond its deserts, some other among the ministerial houses[220] must so envy this success— unless a counselor-class house[221] feels similar envy—that it has concocted slander and false rumor about mine in order to bring it down. However, Heaven discerns every truth, nor could any lie long deceive His Majesty. Obedient to his command, I shall therefore present myself at the Palace Guard office and await his perspicacious judgment regarding my guilt or innocence."

"That is all very well," the imperial officers objected, "but he has obviously hidden Toshisue somewhere. Scour the premises!"

Several thousand warriors burst into the residence, broke into the ceiling and the *nurigome*, pulled down blinds and standing curtains, and left no nook or cranny unexplored. The musicians, who had their instruments tuned for what had promised to be an imperial excursion to view the autumn leaves, fled in all directions without even removing their formal robes. Many of the clerics and laymen, men and women, who had crowded in to witness the spectacle were arrested as suspicious characters and subjected to harsh, wholly unexpected punishment. The imperial troops searched every crack between the rocks of the nearby hills, just in case, but when they found no sign of Toshisue they had to fall back on arresting Kinmune and Bunhira before returning to the capital during the night.

At Sadahira's residence Kinmune was closely confined in a room converted almost into a prison cage.[222] Bunhira was entrusted to Yūki

---

[219] Saionji Kinhira, the older brother of Go-Daigo's late empress Kishi, was Kinmune's grandfather.

[220] *Seiga no ie*, houses just below the *sekkanke* (a *sekkanke* head might become regent), from which a minister (*daijin*) or chancellor (*daijōdaijin*) might be appointed.

[221] *Meika*, a house the head of which might rise to grand counselor (*dainagon*).

[222] *Semerō*, a cell only barely big enough to contain the prisoner.

Chikamitsu[223] and tortured for three straight days and nights. Once he had confessed, he was dragged out to the Rokujō riverbank and beheaded. A council of court nobles ordered Nagatoshi to banish Kinmune to the province of Izumo. Kinmune was to start into exile the following day.

Sadahira conveyed the sentence to Kinmune's wife that night, once it had been pronounced. In tears she stole away in her carriage to visit her husband. She briefly had the guards dismissed and peered into his prison. It was one bay square. Caught in a web of ropes that barred all access to him, he could neither stand nor lie, and his tears of despair so overflowed his sleeves that he could almost have floated away.

He glanced at his wife, wept the more, and said not a word. "What can possibly have brought you to this?" she asked. Dissolved in tears herself, she collapsed and pulled her robe over her head.[224]

After a brief silence Kinmune restrained his weeping and said, "Like a boat adrift with no one at the oars I have sunk to being implicated in a grave crime, and meanwhile I gather that you are expecting. The mere thought that grief over my fate may bring affliction upon you will, I know, insure that I wander in darkness to the next world. If you have a son, do not abandon hope for his future, but bring him up with love and care. He will succeed to our house and stand as a constant reminder of the father he never knew." From the amulet bag kept against his skin he took the score for the secret biwa pieces *Shōgen*, *Ryūsen*, and *Takuboku*. He then handed it to his wife after drawing a nearby inkstone to him and writing this poem on the cover:

> *aware nari*   Ah, it is too hard!
> *hikage matsu ma no*   dewdrop that I am, whose end
> *tsuyu no mi ni*   must come with the sun,

---

[223] Chikamitsu's death, early the following year, is recounted in *Baishōron* ("Takauji's Entry into Kyoto and Yūki Chikamitsu's Worthy Service").

[224] In *gunki monogatari* writing, no wife in dire distress ever does anything else. Perhaps one need not always take the convention seriously.

> *omoi okaruru*　　　　a new worry burdens me:
> *nadeshiko no hana*　　the fate that awaits my child.

The words were difficult to read, so thoroughly had his tears diluted the ink, and she almost fainted at the sight of them. This was to be her last memento of him, however, and he gave it to her weeping afresh. Overwhelmed, she could not speak. She only wept, her gaze to the floor.

A guard then entered. "We are to deliver you tonight to Nagatoshi, the Governor of Hōki," he announced. "At dawn we are to take you to your place of banishment." There was immediately a great deal of coming and going.

Kinmune's wife withdrew from sight and peered out through the woven bamboo fence, sick with worry about what might be in store for her husband. Two or three hundred armed men, summoned by Nagatoshi to take charge of him, were arrayed in the garden. Amid cries of "Hurry, the night is passing!" they dragged him on a rope toward the middle gate. No words could describe her feelings as she watched. A palanquin waited in the garden to receive him, its blinds up. He was about to board it when Sadahira turned to Nagatoshi and said, "Now!"[225] Nagatoshi recognized the order to strike. He rushed to Kinmune, seized his sidelocks, forced him to the ground, drew a dagger, and cut off his head. The crime of an inferior who kills his superior is terrifying to imagine. Kinmune's wife saw it happen. She screamed and collapsed against the fence. Her women thought she had died. They helped her into her carriage and, weeping, started her home toward Kitayama.

---

[225] "Now!" translates *haya*, which might also be rendered, "Quick!" or "Do it!" (The *haya haya toku toku* in the *Kanda-bon*, the oldest surviving *Taiheiki* text, simply repeats "Quick!" four times.) It has been suggested (Keene, *Seeds in the Heart*, p. 846) that Sadahira only wants Nagatoshi to get Kinmune into the palanquin as quickly as possible. However, so colossal a misunderstanding by a subordinate, followed unhesitatingly by such drastic action, is not believable. In principle a man of Kinmune's rank could be subjected to no worse punishment than exile, but in practice those times are gone, as they were already for Narichika in *Heike monogatari* 2. Nagatoshi acts, *kokoroete* that he has been given the order to kill. *Kokoroete* does not mean that he *thinks* he has been ordered to kill when in fact he has not. Rather, he *knows* what the order means.

The crowd of young male and female servants gathered inside and outside the mansion had fled, there was no knowing where. Not one remained. The blinds and standing curtains were all torn down. She looked into the room where he had spent most of his time. Poem slips (*tanzaku*) that he had left there, inscribed with verses written on moonlit nights or snowy mornings, as the spirit moved him, lay scattered far and wide. Now they only reminded her of her loss, and she wept to see them. She looked into the sleeping room. Their bedding lay there as before, but not the husband whose pillow had stood beside hers. His memory lived, but never again would she know the solace of conversation with him. Fallen autumn leaves strewed the garden, and the wind evoked many sorrows. From an old branch, an owl cried eerily into a desolate dawn.

She was wondering how to go on living when a number of young manservants arrived and set about taking the proper dispositions now that (so they explained) Kinshige had been granted the whole of the Saionji family property. This was a further blow. Kinmune's wife moved to a discreet dwelling near Ninnaji.

At last her time came. On the hundredth day after her husband's death she gave birth without difficulty to a little boy. In the old days, alas, holy priests would have been there to pray and to rejoice in her easy delivery. The congratulatory invocation would have been pronounced, and her son would have received his birth-gift of a toy treasure. The news would have spread throughout the land, and horses and carriages would have crowded to her gate. As it was, however, there was no one even to draw the mulberry bow;[226] nor, in her poverty-stricken dwelling (*abaraya*), was there even anywhere to shoot the *yomogi* arrows. Chilling drafts blew through the cracks, so little hindered by any sheltering grove[227] that her son could not even have a wetnurse. No one but his mother herself was there to hold and nurture him. She saw as he grew that he more and more resembled his father.

---

[226] For the birth of a boy, arrows fletched with *yomogi* leaves were shot in the four directions. with a mulberry-wood bow.

[227] Translates for intelligible meaning a phrase quoted from a poem in *Genji* ("Kiritsubo"). She has no protector, no *ushiromi*.

katami koso	This keepsake of his
ima wa ada nare	has become my enemy.
kore naku wa	If it were elsewhere,
wasururu toki mo	I might have at least some hope
aramashi mono o	one day of forgetting him.[228]

So someone had written in times gone by, and the memory of the poem only started fresh tears. Bitter thoughts filled her breast, and the mat in her birthing room never dried.

A messenger from Sadahira brought her this: "His Majesty has inquired about the birth. If you have had a son, he wishes the child's nurse to bring him straight to the palace."

"How awful!" the lady cried. "I did indeed hear that he might wish to search my very entrails for a son of my late husband, and apparently word of my boy's birth is now out. To me, in my sorrow, he is the keepsake my husband left me, and I have been meaning to make a monk of him once he is grown, so as to have him pray for his departed father. And now, if I were to learn that my little child, still at the breast, had fallen into warrior hands and been killed, that grief, heaped upon my previous loss, would render this dewdrop life of mine utterly unbearable. Life is short and hard enough as it is, and it is very bitter indeed to be subjected to such horrors as this!" With these words she dissolved in tears.

Kasuga no Tsubone [Kinmune's mother] went out, weeping, to speak to the messenger. "A son of the late Grand Counselor was indeed born," she said, "but his mother had suffered so greatly during her pregnancy that he passed away soon afterwards. Considering the father's crime, His Majesty may suspect that she is hiding him for fear of the treatment he might receive should he come to His Majesty's attention; and for that reason she is prepared to swear before all the Buddhas and Gods that I speak the truth."

Weeping, she wrote out this statement in a letter, to which she added at the end:

---

[228] *Ise monogatari* 119; translation from Mostow and Tyler, *The Ise Stories*, University of Hawai'i Press, 2010, pp. 239-240.

itsuwari o	No falsehood escapes
tadasu no mori ni	the god of Tadasu Grove
oku tsuyu no	I call to witness:
kieshi ni tsukete	My dewdrop darling is gone,
nururu sode kana	and all I can do is weep.

The messenger took the letter back to Sadahira, who all but wept himself when he read it. His Majesty must have been equally moved, for no further attempt was made to find the child.

Greatly relieved, the lady nonetheless remained as cautious as a mother pheasant tending her chicks in a tussock spared by the flames of a burning field. To prevent anyone ever hearing him cry she kept her hand over his mouth when he nursed at her breast, and she wept silently day and night as she lay beside him.

So three years passed amid sorrows painful to imagine. Then, during Kenmu, conflict broke out, and the Shogun came to govern the realm. The lady's son served the court and succeeded to the Saionji house. He was the Kitayama Right Commander, Lord Sanetoshi.[229]

Actually, an omen had foreshadowed the late Grand Counselor's end. Remarkably enough, Takashige, the Director of the Office of Carpentry, was there to hear it.

At the start of his rebellious plot Lord Kinmune went on a seven-day retreat at Kitano to pray for success, and each night he played secret biwa pieces.[230] Late on the last night, with a cold breeze blowing beneath an awesome moon, he had his blinds raised high and—presumably for the particular pleasure of the holy spirit enshrined there—played the prelude to *Gyokuju sanjo*.

> The first and second strings gust and rage
> like wind blustering through autumn pines;

---

[229] Sanetoshi served the Northern Court and rose through grand counselor to right minister at senior second rank, as related in *Taiheiki* 30 and later.

[230] The Saionji heads had special knowledge of the biwa, which, as *Masukagami* shows, they often played in imperial concerts (*asobi*).

> the third and fourth cry out mournfully,
> like a caged crane by night calling her child.[231]

The smothered urgency of the music[232] propelled a rhythm that, repeated six times, could have brought a babe in arms to his feet to dance.

Takashige happened then to be on night vigil at the shrine, and he lent the music an attentive ear. He remarked when it was over, "If the Grand Counselor meant his biwa music tonight as a prayer, that prayer will fail. I refer to the piece entitled *Gyokuju*. Long ago, when King Ping Gong of Jin passed by the river Pu, the flowing water made a sound like pipes and strings. Ping Gong summoned a musician named Shi Juan and had him transcribe this sound into music for the *kin*. The resulting piece sounded so sad that all who heard it wept. Nonetheless Ping Gong liked it very much and had it played often. When the musician Shi Kuang heard it, he criticized it to the king.

"'If you so favor this piece the realm will fall,' he said, 'and the ancestral mausolea will lie in ruins. Why? When of old King Zhou of Yin came to favor such sad music, he was soon destroyed by King Wu of Zhou. His spirit lingered at the bottom of the river Pu, making that same music, which you then had made into a new piece and favored in turn. The music of Zheng corrupts genuine music. It is no music to perform, still less to praise.' In the end, Ping Gong came to naught, but the music lived thereafter until the age of Chen. Shu Bao, the last king of Chen, loved it and was destroyed by Sui. Emperor Yang of Sui loved it passionately and was destroyed by Tai Zong of Tang.

"Toward the end of the Tang a Japanese musician, Sadatoshi, the Director of Palace Maintenance,[233] crossed the sea as ambassador to China, met the great Chinese biwa master Lian Chengwu, and brought this music back to our land. He omitted one particular passage as excessively ill-omened, but the Grand Counselor's musical offering

---

[231] Lines by Bo Juyi on the five-string biwa, *Wakan rōei shū* 463. They seem to be quoted here in order to explain the effect of the music.

[232] An expression derived from the line on the fifth string: "The fifth string's voice is the most thoroughly smothered: the River Lu, frozen, groans, unable to flow."

[233] The fourth son of Fujiwara no Fuhito. He was appointed ambassador to China in 845.

tonight purposely included it and gave it a particularly menacing tone. I was appalled. Music is continuous with government. The Grand Counselor is sure to suffer misfortune of some kind." So Takashige spoke, sorrowfully. Indeed, all too soon Kinmune was executed. This was an extraordinary omen.

TAKEMUKI-GA-KI

BOOK TWO
Late 1337 to ca. 1351

36
Sanetoshi's First Taste of Fish

This year [Kenmu 4, 1337] my son [3rd year] had his First Taste of Fish (*mana hajime*).[234] On 12.21 he moved to the Right Minister's residence.[235] [Hino] officials and housemen accompanied him, and two gentle-women shared his carriage. They brought a box lid (*hirobuta*)[236] lined with two sheets of *usuyō* paper and containing his sword, his *amagatsu*,[237] five double-layered *kosode*, and many other things. He wore:

akome[238]

suō no karaorimono (kameishi-datami)   maroon
ornamented sash [jewels, gold, silver]
aoki hitoe   ao green
triple kosode (kameishi-datami)   white, kameishi pattern

There was also a display carriage. The Right Minister wore *eboshi* and *nōshi*. I gather that the household officials and housemen, for years cut off from the world came forward eagerly to welcome him. The Minister assured me that everything about my son visibly augured well for his future. Apparently the fifty-day and hundred-day celebrations[239] are now to go forward.

There is no peace in the world, but the [Jimyōin] line, which faced extinction, has now been renewed. That is wonderful. My father shares in this glory and now towers in standing above all others.[240]

---

[234] The solemn first feeding of adult food.
[235] The former right minister Tōin Kinkata, a Saionji and the author of *Entairyaku*.
[236] A broad, square, shallow container for such things as clothing.
[237] A doll meant to absorb any evil influence that might harm a small child. Child and doll were inseparable.
[238] *Eriki no tame akome o mochiiru.* The meaning of *eriki* is unknown.
[239] Celebrations following the birth, postponed because of what had happened to Kinmune.
[240] Sukena, in his fifty-first year, was Kōmyō's foster father.

37
The Hino Residence Burns

So time went by, until on 3.19 [Kenmu 5, 1338], fire broke out in the middle of the night. I was living some distance from where it started, but there was still was no escape. I dropped everything and fled. Everyone gathered in a little building to the north. I thought I was dreaming. It was horrifying.

The preparations under way to receive the newborn Prince[241] were abandoned. Thereafter the northern and southern plots of land were merged, and soon work was under way day and night to make the lake and garden knolls just as handsome as they could be. The idea was that the Prince should come once the work was finished, but his father was so keen for the move to proceed that the Prince arrived in the 4th month.[242]

---

[241] Iyahito (born Kenmu 5.3.2), Kōgon's second son and the future Emperor Go-Kōgon. Sukena was his foster father as well.

[242] To the quarters occupied by Sukena.

38
The Death of Sukena

About the 20th of that month Lady Nii went on retreat to the Kitakōji Nenbutsu,[243] and I gladly took the opportunity to join her. Then, to my dismay, my father suddenly became unwell. I was about to leave when he seemed to improve a little. I therefore stayed where I was, since he seemed to be suffering from only a passing indisposition. Then at dawn on 5.2 a man came running to fetch me, saying that his condition had deteriorated during the night and that he appeared unlikely to recover. There was nothing to say. Confusion and dismay pervaded the household. The ministrations of the attending physicians did no good. He passed away last at the hour of the sheep [2 p.m.]. Our feelings defied description. My mother renounced the world that very day.[244] This sudden disaster brought the fragility of life painfully home to me.

During the bardo (*chūin*) period[245] a throng of monks conducted services throughout the six hours of day and night. That was sad and troubling enough, but, in addition, toward the end distasteful issues arose over the succession to the Saionji house, and to my dismay prayers to encourage a happy rebirth seemed to take second place. Both the Prince and the young Adviser [Sanetoshi] spent that time at Lady Nii's home.[246]

---

[243] The wife of Saionji Sanehira joins the gathering to invoke Amida, probably at the Senbon Shakadō (Daihōonji) at Ichijō-Kitakōji.

[244] No pronoun or anything like one identifies Nako's mother, probably the "Shiba Nun" who appears later in the memoir.

[245] The first forty-nine days after death.

[246] Presumably the Saionji residence on Imadegawa.

39
Sanetoshi's Trimming-of-the-Hair

Ryakuō 2 [1339] arrived. The former Right Minister,[247] who had been unwell, passed away in the first month of the year. This was a great and sad loss. Grave complications had arisen over the Saionji succession, but nothing came of them.

This was the year for my son's trimming-of-the-hair (*fukasogi*).[248] I was thinking of discussing the matter with Eifukumon-in when I heard that she wished to see it done before the end of the year. That suited me perfectly. She therefore repaired to Kitayama on 12.28. Lady Nii accompanied her, together with many gentlewomen. My son wore:

double *kōbai akome, karaori*	plum pink
aoki hitoe	*ao* green
triple *kosode, shiroki karaori*	white

They would have been sorry to hurry straight back again, and Eifukumon-in expressed a wish to greet the New Year here. She therefore decided on the spur of the moment to stay on and left only the next day. She declared herself pleased to have found my son even more promising than she had imagined. According to Lady Nii she had wanted to know all about the garden brook—where it came from and where it went—and had been delighted to find him, so far, remarkable. As a gift she left me a scroll in the hand of Retired Emperor Fushimi, attached to an artificial sprig of pine.[249]

---

247 Kikutei (Imadegawa) Kanesue.

248 A child in his third to fifth year has his long hair ceremonially trimmed and tidied. Sanetoshi is in his fifth year.

249 Fushimi was the father of Go-Fushimi and Hanazono. This would have been a scroll of copied waka. Many scrolls or fragments in Fushimi's hand survive. This one may have been meant as a calligraphy model for Nako's son.

40
The Pilgrimage to Tennōji

In the middle of the 2nd month [Ryakuō 3, 1340] I went on pilgrimage, suitably accompanied, to Tennōji. A boat awaited us at Mitsu-no-mimaki.[250] We were to make a particular stop on the way. At Naniwa all agreed that it might be dangerous to venture onto the sea in a river boat, and indeed the waves were so high when we reached the sea that the prospect looked very different. I had never traveled like this before, and everything was quite new to me. After nightfall we reached a grubby inn. There was hardly time to nap a little before we set off, late in the night, to stop at the crossing to Ashiya. The shore wind had blown hard and cold as the day waned, but perhaps even so it was a sign of spring[251] that a misty moon shone far across the sea.

The image (*tameshi*) of an unmoored boat, adrift, was certainly moving.[252] The ancient little house we stayed in, roofed with reeds, was not "thatched in many layers,"[253] which may explain why moonlight shone through in many places. At dawn we rose to leave, and I enjoyed leaving this behind:

yado toite	What new traveler
tare mata koyoi	will come here again, tonight,
kusamakura	in need of shelter
karine no yume o	and, caught up in restless sleep,
musubi kasanen	dream other dreams, her own?

The others staying there boarded little fishing boats and set off, each a different way. I wondered sympathetically where they were all going.

---

[250] Mitsu is Yodo in present Fushimi-ku, Kyoto, on the west bank of the Kizu-gawa. Mimaki may be either a common noun or an element of the place name.

[251] "A sign of spring" (*haru no shirube*) is from a poem by Minamoto no Toshiyori (*Horikawa hyakushu* 88, also *Sanboku kikashū* 41). Typically for a travel account this passage alludes several times to earlier waka and shows the influence of poems by Emperor Fushimi and Saionji Sanekane. Nako's grandfather, Toshimitsu, was a member of Fushimi's poetry circle, and his *Toshimitsu shū* was one of the materials drawn on by Reizei Tamekane for the *Gyokuyō shū*.

[252] An allusion to a Chinese poem by Luo Wei (*Wakan rōei shū* 760) and also to a passage in the "Hahakigi" chapter of *Genji monogatari* (Tyler, *The Tale of Genji*, p. 26).

[253] From *Goshūishū* 69, by Izumi Shikibu.

yo no hodo mo	For a single night,
tomari wa onaji	all of us lodged together.
tabine tote	Now we travelers
yomo ni wakaruru	go each our separate ways
oki no tsuribune	on fishing boats, over the sea.

During my leisurely stay at Tennōji I made a pilgrimage to Sumiyoshi. Whatever they may call the plants that grow there on the shore,[254] I envied the waves that broke and returned to the sea, pondering meanwhile many things in my longing to recover days gone by. I shudder to imagine what the divinity may have thought of me.

---

[254] They are called *wasuregusa* ""grasses of forgetting" (*Kokinshū* 1111 and *Shūishū* 888).

41
Sanetoshi Moves to Kitayama

In Ryakuō 3.5 [1340] I heard that Senseimon-in[255] had renounced the world in the Ninnaji dwelling of the Honorary Empress.[256] This was shocking news.[257]

On the 6th the Tōbokuin Grand Prelate (*sōjō*)[258] became ill, and on the 19th he passed away like morning dew. No words can convey the sorrow of this loss.

Meanwhile, Eifukumon-in prepared to receive the young Adviser [Sanetoshi, at Kitayama]. I was to come with him, which seemed reasonable enough, but I silently wondered how things might go if I did. Through Lady Nii I therefore raised the matter with Eifukumon-in. She naturally replied that my fears were quite unjustified and that there was no question of estranging him from me, so I weakly gave in and agreed. Lady Nii accompanied me briefly.[259] My gentlewomen came with me. They connected the Kogosho for me to the Takemuki pavilion. Everything was as it had been, and much of the past came back. The Grand Counselor's[260] officials and housemen, who had been lost and idle without him, saw at last a revival of their fortunes. Decrepit old novices and the like came forward once more to be of service, and their visible faith in one whom they saw as their lord was

---

[255] In the original, Shin Nyōin, "the new nyōin." Senseimon-in is her *ingō*. She is Princess Kanshi (1313-1362), a daughter of Go-Daigo who, in her nineteenth year (Genkō 3.12) became one of Kōgon's women.

[256] Unidentified.

[257] It indeed appalled Ichijō Tsunemichi (*Gyokueishō* for Ryakuō 3.5.30 [1340]), who found her dereliction of duty inexcusable, despite the many indignities that she had suffered.

[258] Kakuen (1275-1340), superintendent (*bettō*) of Kōfukuji, son of Saionji Sanekane, and brother of Saionji Kinhira and Eifukumon-in. His death may well have facilitated Sanetoshi's move to Kitayama.

[259] Since the formal wife of the previous house head could not live indefinitely in the main residence with the formal wife of the current one, Ujiko (Lady Nii, the wife of Saionji Sanehira) can stay only briefly.

[260] Nako does not identify her late husband. His title of grand counselor is supplied here to make it clear to whom she refers.

touching to behold. I kept wishing that things had gone differently for them.

The Adviser should properly have inhabited the North Pavilion,[261] but Eifukumon-in insisted on having him nearby, and he settled immediately into the South Pavilion. She kept him beside her day and night, far more so than I had ever imagined her doing, and in all ways showered attentions upon him.

One snowy morning, when his people were having him read his daily classics lesson,[262] he made this poem:

yuki furite	Here it is snowing
samuki ashita ni	on this freezing cold morning,
fumi yome to	and they still insist
semeraruru koso	that I must read my lesson.
kanashū wa are	O it is just too hard!

Eifukumon-in heard about this:

fumisomuru	These, his first words
waka no koshiji no	upon on the everlasting
tori no ato ni	path of poetry
nao mo taesenu	encourage abundant hope
sue o miekeru	that he will yet go far.

And on another snowy morning she sent:

sakaubeki	For what years to come
yado no aruji no	will the master of a house
ikutose ka	destined for glory
taenu miyuki no	welcome, snow upon snow,
ato o mirubeki	the visits of our sovereigns?[263]
kenu ga ue ni	When upon deep snow
furitsumu yuki no	fresh snow falls, lovelier yet,
nasake ni mo	surely you, like me,

---

[261] As the head of the Saionji house.

[262] *Fumi*, the Chinese classics.

[263] The play on *miyuki*, "imperial progress" and "snow," underlies this poem. Even without the explicit double meaning, *yuki* ("snow") implies the same thing in other poems, for example those in no. 46.

yado no aruji o	anticipate eagerly
matsu to shirazu ya	a new master of our house.[264]

---

[264] A poem inspired by *Kokinshū* 333.

42
A Directional Taboo

Late that year a directional taboo required the Retired Emperor [Kōgon] to move elsewhere. He went to the residence of Eifukumon-in, but it was up to the host's house to provide the hospitality required. The host [Sanetoshi] called on the RE in a *moegi* green *suikan* (*karaorimono*). The next day, the RE looked into the southern garden and saw a row of icicles hanging like jewels from the eaves of Muryōkō-in.[265] Apparently struck by the sight, he had one collected, then called for an inkstone box lid, lined it with a *kōri-gasane* of *usuyō* paper, and showed it off [to Eifukumon-in]. He had the blinds raised in the west room of the main house, and wine was served. A large branch of the pine beside the open gallery having broken under the weight of snow, the break had been cut smooth. The RE asked what had happened, and Sanetoshi promptly told him. The RE was delighted. "A fine answer from my host!" he declared. That was pleasing to hear. The RE served him wine in his own cup and seems to have made a great fuss over him. The Grand Counselor, the Sanjō Counselor,[266] and various Privy Gentlemen were present.

---

[265] The main hall of Saionji, the chief temple on the Kitayama estate.
[266] Kikutei (Imadegawa) Sanetada, a son of Kanesue, and Sanjō Sanetsugu.

43
Kianmon-in's First Visit to Kitayama

In Ryakuō 4.4 [1341] the Hagiwara-dono Princess entered Jimyōin House.[267] She immediately received the title (*ingō*) of Kianmon-in. Her first visit came in the 8ᵗʰ month. She was to stay, just across from here,[268] with Eifukumon-in. The Retired Emperor came too, and his host [Sanetoshi] therefore called on them. I was very pleased to gather that the RE had remarked to Eifukumon-in, "I am delighted to see that he promises so well for the future," and so on.

---

[267] Princess Hisako, a daughter of Hanazono and Senkōmon-in Saneko—herself a daughter of Ōgimachi Saneaki. She became Kōgon-in's *kisaki*. He had no *chūgū*.
[268] In the Kitayama southern pavilion, where Sanetoshi lives.

44
The Kasuga Sacred Tree's Return to Nara

The Sacred Tree (*shinboku*), which had been at the Chōkōdō, returned in the 9th month,[269] accompanied by Fujiwara gentlemen. The Regent,[270] Ministers, and Senior Nobles walked in procession. The Chief Priest[271] carried it. This supremely solemn event proceeded with the utmost splendor. Suenori[272] looked after the viewing stands. Eifukumon-in came, too. There were many display carriages, and everyone from the main house was there. By great good fortune the Tree returned to the Shrine without incident.

---

[269] In Ryakuō 3.12 [1340], Kōfukuji monks had brought the sacred *sakaki* of the Kasuga Shrine to the Chōkōdō, as so often, to press a grievance. The issue was apparently settled, and the tree returned to the shrine on Ryakuō 4.8.19. (Nako's "9th month" seems to be an error.)

[270] Ichijō Tsunemichi.

[271] Ōnakatomi Morotoshi.

[272] Probably a Saionji retainer.

45
Go-Fushimi's Daughter Goes to Kitayama

The Retired Emperor spoke of having his daughter come here.[273] People objected that there was absolutely no precedent for such a thing, but he kept insisting. Eifukumon-in therefore suggested that the young lady simply be thought of as coming to live with her. Accordingly, she arrived in the 10th month.

---

[273] Implying marriage to Sanetoshi. The daughter has not been identified. A few imperial daughters had "married down" (*kōka*) into a regental house (*sekke* or *sekkanke*), but never into the Saionji, one step lower.

46
Sanetoshi Comes of Age

On 12.7 of that year my son came of age (*genbuku*). For the occasion the west end of the main house was joined to the Ōki pavilion.[274] The blinds of a bay on the south side were raised. Two bays were given over to the Senior Nobles: the Sono Counselor (Lord Motonari), the Sanjō Counselor (Lord Sanetsugu), and the Chief of Police (*bettō*) Sukeaki. They wore *nōshi* tied low (*ge-kukuri*). In the next bay, straw mats were laid over the board floor. The sliding panels between the Ōki pavilion and the main house were removed and blinds hung in their place. This is where Eifukumon-in sat. The sponsor (*kakan*) sat the edge of the blinds to the east, above the Senior Nobles.[275]

One bay on the north side of the building was set aside for the donning of the *hakama* (*chako*). The blinds there were raised and tall lamps (*takatōdai*) set in place. He donned the *hakama* there, wearing:

suikan: urakoki suō (*karaorimono, tsurubishi pattern*)	maroon
moegi no akome (*matsudasuki* pattern)	*moegi* green
kōbai no ukiorimono no kosode	plum pink
shiro orimono hada kosode (same pattern as *suikan*)	white

He then changed into the Retired Emperor's *nōshi* and *sashinuki*.[276] The costume master was Shigetō.[277] The Grand Counselor[278] tied the *hakama* cords. The utensils for the ceremonial meal were silver. The meal was served by Tomoo. Three household officials (Mitsuhira, Nagahira, and Kazuhira) brought it in.

He examined the propitious writ (*kissho*).[279] Next, he sat on a straw mat while another was

---

[274] Unknown.

[275] The sponsor placed the headdress of manhood on the young person's head. He may have been Kikutei Sanetada.

[276] Gifts from Kōgon.

[277] Surname unknown; a yin-yang master, specializing also in costume, who had served Saionji Kinhira.

[278] Probably Kikutei Sanetada.

[279] A felicitous document read by a young man coming of age, as a testament to his

spread for the gentleman who was to dress his hair. The RE's headdress (*kōburi*) was placed to his right. The official in this case was Tomoo. Then another official (Kazuhira) placed the water vessel (*yusurutsuki*)[280] to his left. The utensils lay in an accessory box. Opinions differ as to whether the comb towel (*kushi tanagoi*) should go over or under them, but it this case it went over. The Sono Chamberlain Captain then came forward to dress the hair, wearing *sokutai*. The sponsor placed the RE's headdress on the head of my son, who stepped down below the lintel (*nageshi*) and danced his formal thanks (*hai*). He then returned to where he had donned the *hakama*.

Meanwhile the Chamberlain Captain brought in the gift sword[281] (in a brocade bag), then returned with it whence he had come. Next, Tanekage and Shigekiyo led the horse through the middle gate to the south front of the building. Suenori held the torch.

When it was all over, my son changed into a *kariginu* in the two-bay gallery (*futamune*): [282]

kariginu: shiro ao	light *ao* green
sashinuki: koki murasaki	dark purple
heiken: harajiro	light purple
shita no hakama	dark purple
suō no akome: double, damask	maroon
hitoe: damask	*moegi* green
sugi no yokome no ōgi	cryptomeria fan
tatōgami: usuyō paper	

Once he was dressed, further refreshments were served in the *hakama* room. The utensils this time were less formal. Of old they would have rested on a length of superior weave, but in this informal setting a relief-patterned weave (*uki-aya*) was used. Likewise, white was adopted for the *fusekumi*.[283] The same people as before brought in the

adulthood.
[280] A vessel on a stand, containing water for dressing the sidelocks.
[281] For the sponsor.
[282] A curtained-off gallery, two bays long, projecting from the *moya* and usable as a separate room.

refreshments and served them. Once that was over, the Senior Nobles and Privy Gentlemen were served wine. A private drinking party followed.

It snowed heavily that night. Very early the next morning the Chief of Police congratulated me, assuring me that the event the previous day had been done superbly and stood up to any in the past.

sakaubeki	That a brilliant future
yukusue kakete	stretches before him,
shirayuki no	the white snow confirms,
furinuru ie ni	falling reign after reign
ato o kasanaru	on his noble heritage.

I added to my reply:

shirayuki no	Where the white snow falls,
furinuru ato mo	there in times yet to come
mata sara ni	shall blossom, assured,
hana to miyubeki	a future as glorious
sue mo tanomoshi	as a perfect flower.

Oh yes, the Shogun [Takauji] presented my son with a horse and a sword. His gift was all the more felicitous because it followed precedent.[284]

---

[283] A kind of ornamental, triple-braided cord.
[284] Presumably a reference to past gifts on felicitous occasions from the shogun to the Saionji house head, who held the office of *Kantō mōshitsugi*.

47
Go-Fushimi's Visit to Kitayama

The spring appointments list named my son a Captain. He was in his eighth year.

The Retired Emperor's first trip this year [Ryakuō 5, 1342] brought him here, to our Kitayama. People apparently remarked, "These imperial honors[285] still recognize their once signal service to the throne." After the coming-of-age, an imperial edict allowed him the forbidden colors: *nōshi* and *sashinuki* of patterned *aya*. The drinking party (*ōmiki*) was private. The horse and ox were presented in the customary manner. The RE inspected them, and suitable Privy Gentlemen led them, as always. The ceremony took place at night. The RE's last visit here had been long ago, and this one felt so remarkable that the prescribed formalities seemed insufficient. We searched the treasury (*hōzō*), found a pair of flower vases[286] (*hanatate*) over three feet tall, and presented them to him. He commented favorably on them, remarking that they were exceptionally beautiful in color and form.

"My host's [Sanetoshi's] manners and deportment promise so well for the future that I am delighted for the sake of both houses, the imperial and the Saionji," the RE said. This was thoroughly gratifying. Later on he expressed the same sentiments repeatedly to Eifukumon-in. His imperial letters were so heartening that I got them from her and kept them.

---

[285] Presumably Sanetoshi's coming-of-age, immediate official appointment, and leave to wear the forbidden colors (*kinjiki*).
[286] For flower offerings on an altar.

48
A Pilgrimage to Ishiyama

The 20th of the 2nd month had passed when I made a discreet pilgrimage to Ishiyama. I assumed that I would eventually cross the Ōsaka barrier again, with all its comings and goings,[287] but such is life that not even tomorrow is assured, and I could not help wondering with some emotion whether this might be the last time after all.[288] At Sekidera[289] they put my palanquin down and gave me a lunch box (*hiwarigo*). The view from there across the lake has always struck me as extraordinary. I arrived near sunset. Since I meant to keep all-night vigil, I left the door facing the altar open and spent the night chanting sutras. The lamp shed only dim light, and there was little sign of human presence. It was all very gloomy and lonely.

They say that the temple's sacred image [290] was cast from gold dust. Apparently Prince Shōtoku had worshiped it in a previous life.

There was no gold anywhere, though, when Emperor Shōmu built Tōdaiji, so prayers were offered, and the priest Rōben received an imperial command to discover the holy site where it might be found. When a purple cloud arose, Rōben made his way toward it, came to this mountain, and saw that the cloud issued from a rock shaped like an eight-petaled lotus. He placed this image on the rock, prayed before it for seven days, and learned that he was to address himself to Zaō of Yoshino. When he did so, a gold nugget the size of a *mari* ball appeared in the Yoshino River. It rolled away from anyone who tried to pick it up, but an imperial envoy who went to the spot successfully took possession of it. So it was that the prayers for gold were answered. The *engi* tells the story at length.[291] Since the image remained on the rock, Rōben made a statue of Guse [also Guze] Kannon and placed the sacred

[287] A expression derived from *Goshūishū* 723 and 724.

[288] An allusion to *Shūishū* 495.

[289] Chōanji in Ōtsu, the setting for the Noh play *Sekidera Komachi*.

[290] According to *Ishiyamadera engi*, a six-inch, two-armed, Kongōzō Nyoirin Kannon worshiped by Emperor Shōmu.

[291] Nako's version of the *Ishiyamadera engi* story differs from any now known, even though the earliest text of the *engi* (Shōchū, 1324-1326) dates from just before her time.

image inside it. Apparently he then curtained off the rock. No doubt this statue is Guse Kannon, since Prince Shōtoku himself was Guse Kannon.

No one knew what the sacred image looked like until fire broke out, and the image flew, shining, into the willow tree before the main hall. Rōben reproduced its form in the willow itself, which is why people still speak of the "copied figure" (*hito utsushi*).[292] Rōben's cell (*bō*) was beneath it. Apparently everything from there to the worship hall (*raidō*)[293] burned, but the main hall survived unchanged from when it was first built. So I was told, and perhaps it is true.

---

[292] The meaning of the original sentence (as of the expression *hito utsushi)* is uncertain. In Tenpyō Hōji 6 (762) Rōben made a *jōroku* (life-size) Nyoirin Kannon statue the same in form as the gold image and placed the gold image inside it. However, the statue burned in Shōryaku 2 (1078), and the present one, made by Eison, dates from Kōan 8 (1285). Perhaps Nako was either confused or misinformed.
[293] The *raidō* stood before the main hall (*hondō*). One worshiped the temple's sacred Kannon image from there.

49
A Pilgrimage to Sakura-dani

The next day I went on pilgrimage to Sakura-dani, where Benzaiten resides.[294] Still in my palanquin, I crossed by boat to the hillside opposite. The place was extremely isolated, even terrifying. At last a shrine servant (*jinnin*)—I believe he was—dressed in yellow appeared. He offered *mitegura*, opened the sanctuary a little, and chanted a *norito* prayer. The river looked very wide, and the constant boiling of the waves, dashing themselves so desperately against the rocks[295] then curling back, looked quite daunting. On the other side of the river is a very high hill, on top of which, I heard, is a splendid shrine.[296]

I decided to return via Hiyoshi. Haze shrouded the Shiga shore when I reached it, and the rising moon seemed to stride through the waves. The Karasaki Pine must have grown old long ago, because it looked very small. Some men were setting out in boats across the lake. I turned right [along the shore] and glanced back toward the left. A vast stretch of wave-washed coast faded into an almost boundless distance, so beautiful that I was sorry to have to pass on by.

---

[294] Sakuradani, the site of Sakunado Jinja, is in the mountains south of Ōtsu, at the confluence of the Ōishi-gawa and the Seto-gawa. Like Nako, the *Kagerō nikki* author mentions it after a pilgrimage to Ishiyama, calling it Sakunadani (Sonja Arntzen, *The Kagerō Diary*, Ann Arbor: Center for Japanese Studies, The University of Michigan, 1997, p. 211; Jacqueline Pigeot, *Mémoires d'une éphémère (954-974)*. Paris: Collège de France, Institut des Hautes Études Japonaises, 2006, p. 98; Inukai Kiyoshi, ed. *Kagerō nikki* (Shinchō Nihon koten shūsei). Shinchōsha, 1982, p. 125). There is no known connection between the place and Benzaiten; rather, *Yakumo mishō* associates it with purification and the entrance to the underworld. The *Kagerō* author's women mention a tradition that no one who enters the ravine ever returns.

[295] An allusion to *Shikashū* 211.

[296] Despite her use of the word *yashiro*, Nako must mean Tachiki-yama and Tachiki Kannon, a temple said to have been founded by Kūkai before he founded Mount Kōya.

50
Memories of the Chōkōdō

In the 3rd month I visited the Wakamiya.[297] The Chōkōdō is visible nearby. I directed my carriage to go there and looked around. Many memories came to mind, such as the flower-offering of old. As I stood under the blossoms, everything seemed the same. It felt as though spring in the world I once knew had come round again, and I so wanted to talk to them about my memories of those days that I even resented their inevitable silence.[298]

One evening at the time of the Eight Lotus Lectures (*mihakō*)[299]— what year can it have been?—the Retired Emperors [Go-Fushimi, Hanazono] were chatting amid a cluster of gentlewomen. There was nobody about. Lady Nii, Saishō no Suke, and others talked of past and present, calling up memories of one person or another, few of whom figured any longer in their world. Some had donned the robe of renunciation and led wholly different lives, or lived otherwise, for good or for ill, in a manner quite unlike what they had once known. This flood of memories brought tears to everyone's eyes.

yado mo sore	There it is, the hall,
hana mo mishi yo no	under trees as then in bloom.
ki no shita ni	Why is it, alas,
nareshi haru nomi	that the spring I knew so well
nado ka tomaranu	has gone, never to return?

The plum tree next to the Memorial Hall (*mieidō*)[300] must not have been pruned, it came so close to the eaves. I looked into where they held the flower offering and remembered with sharp nostalgia those who had sat there side by side. The two pines in the court (*tsubo*) had grown so unrecognizably tall[301] that I almost wondered who I was.[302]

---

[297] The Sameushi Wakamiya Hachimangū, built in Tengi 1 (1050) at Rokujō-Nishinotōin.

[298] An allusion to *Wakan rōeishū* 117 and *Goshūishū* 130.

[299] A solemn, four-day Lotus Sutra ritual often performed in the Chōkōdō.

[300] For Go-Shirakawa (1127-1192).

[301] An allusion to *Gosenshū* 1107.

[302] The expression *ware ya aranu* varies on the *tsuki ya aranu* of Narihira's most

People have told me that Retired Emperor Fushimi personally planted them as seedlings.

On my way back I passed the main hall's privy chamber.[303] One quiet night, at the time of the Lotus Confession (*gosenbō*)[304] long ago, the Retired Emperor [Go-Fushimi] was wondering where his gentlemen had got to when he heard that Grand Prelate (*sōjō*) Sojū,[305] on duty in the back room, was entertaining a group of *chigo*. It was a dark night. He took only me with him to the side door and peered in. There the Grand Prelate was, apparently disporting himself with great abandon, since the RE made an acrostic poem (*oriku*) with the initial letters *cha-ya-su-ko-shi*;[306] asked me to write it out in katakana, which I did on a sheet of thin *sakura* paper;[307] and had me slip it inside the door attached to a willow sprig.[308]

"What is *this* about?" the Prelate asked through one of the *chigo*, while the others all wondered aloud who it could be from. They never imagined it being from the RE. Eventually the Prelate grasped the truth, and sent him wine and tea presented with the greatest elegance. That night the gentlemen therefore summoned Kōwaka, Ato, and the others, and enjoyed an impromptu entertainment. The wit of this otherwise insignificant incident perfectly conveys my memory of him in those days.

---

famous poem (*Kokinshū* 747, *Ise monogatari* 4).

[303] Where court officials on duty gathered as required.

[304] A rite that involved chanting the Lotus Sutra and confessing sins.

[305] Unknown; perhaps an error for Jijū, mentioned in no. 18 as head monk of Yokawa and Hosshōji.

[306] "A spot of tea, please."

[307] *Sakura usuyō*. As a layering (*kasane*) *sakura* is variously explained. Presumably it conveys white with the faintest flush of pink.

[308] Presumably the monk and the boys were playing *tōcha*, a game popular at the time. It involved distinguishing different varieties of tea, especially *honcha* (tea from Toganoo) and *hicha* (tea from anywhere else).

51
A Gift from Takauji

The Kamakura Gentleman of the Second Rank [Takauji] was acquainted with this house and therefore wrote from time to time. During Ryakuō [1338.8 to 1342.4] the usual succession issue arose, and there was some correspondence with him on the subject. In the 4th month some goose eggs came from him, and we in turn sent him several tens, tied together and attached to wisteria boughs. Eifukumon-in wrote on the *usuyō* paper that lined the box lid:

tori no ko o	More than those ten eggs
tō zutsu too no	multiplied in stacked-up tens
kazu yori mo	make a great many,
omou omoi wa	my fond heart cherishes hopes
masari koso seme	beyond counting for this boy.[309]

<hr>

[309] Hopes for the Saionji house and Sanetoshi. The poem draws on one in *Ise monogatari* 50 (tr. in Mostow and Tyler, *The Ise Stories*, p. 112) and another in *Kagerō nikki* (tr. in Arntzen, *The Kagerō Diary,* p. 143).

52
Kinmune's Dreamed Poem

At about the same time Azechi no Nii[310] wrote, "Someone dreamed of the departed and heard him say this. I wonder what bitterness moved him. It made me so sad." This was his poem:

omoi oku	Never mind just now
sore o ba okite	the point that most vexes me:
koto no ha no	what I want to know
tsuyu no nasake no	is why I should never have
nado ka nakaruran	one word of sympathy.

I suspected that he resented the attitude of the other side,[311] and I mourned him more deeply than ever.

---

[310] Perhaps the daughter of Shimizudani Nagatsugu, attached to Hanazono-in.
[311] Nako's husband's half brother Kinshige and his sympathizers, in the struggle for the Saionji house.

53
The Death of Eifukumon-in

I had already gathered that Eifukumon-in was unwell, although without marked symptoms, when in late spring she became unmistakably ill. I was extremely upset. Her condition worsened daily. The Retired Emperor [Kōgon] and Kianmon-in came to see her, and she asked Kianmon-in to look after the Captain [Sanetoshi]. It was all extremely painful.

She passed away on the 7th of the 5th month [of Kōei 1, 1342]. Having always looked to her in every matter, day or night, I felt grief beyond words. As for what remained to be done, she had arranged everything beforehand with the temple at Iwakura.[312] Her journey there on the 8th emulated a living progress. Lord Chikurin-in [Kinshige] received her palanquin. Everyone was appalled. To think that even at the very last she should have been subjected to anything so distressing![313] Apparently the Sanjō-bōmon Grand Counselor [Nakanoin Michifuyu] had been asked to do it and had agreed, but then a sudden difficulty had intervened. The priests looked after everything, and we had no bardo services (*chūin no gi*)[314] here. People were shocked that she had preferred to forego ceremony on so weighty an occasion. I bitterly regretted that her son had gone before her, reflecting how different things would have been if only the late Cloistered Emperor [Go-Fushimi, 1288-1336] had been alive.

Her gentlewomen continued in her service as before during the seven times seven days;[315] then, with renewed tears, all dispersed. Only Uemon-no-tsubone stayed on in her Privy Chamber room (*tenjō no tsubone*).[316] Later she moved to a village nearby, as though to honor the memory of what had been.

---

[312] Daiunji, a Tendai temple in present Sakyo-ku, Iwakura, Agura-chō.

[313] Kinshige's claim to succeed to Kinmune as head of the Saionji house was making things at Kitayama extremely unpleasant, and Eifukumon-in opposed him.

[314] Buddhist services performed every seven days for the first forty-nine days, to guide the departed toward a good rebirth. Below, "the seven days."

[315] The original has *go-shichinichi no hodo*, "during the seven days," but it is likely that one "seven" is missing.

[316] Presumably next to Eifukumon-in at Kitayama.

54
Sanetoshi's Thanks for His Appointment as Captain

On 7.25 Sanetoshi rendered formal thanks for his promotion to Captain. The sky was particularly clear, and the breeze was cool. The prognostication for the day and hour was submitted,[317] and prayers for good health (*migatame*) were performed by the yin-yang masters Akinatsu and Matanari. Mitsuhira oversaw the arrangements that day and the previous one. The Palace Guards provided five escorts (*zuijin*), six junior attendants (*kozōshiki*), and two senior guards (*bangashira*). This house provided three escorts, two household officials (*shotaifu*) (Mitsuhira and Nagahira), five[318] housemen (*saburai*) (Mitsutomo, Kageyori, Zenryō, Iemune, Sanemori, Tokishige), and an ox driver in a starched white *kariginu* (*joboku*). The Ichijō Captain accompanied him in his carriage.

He went first to Jimyōin House. The Retired Emperor's [Kōgon's] gift was a biwa (Yōyū, which he had received from Saionji Sanekane). From Kianmon-in he received a flute (in a bag). On the way he stopped at Lady Nii's Ichijō-Imadegawa residence, then went on to the palace. He did his best to get there before sunset, but the sun was down by the time he arrived. Spectators lined the streets in carriages and even in palanquins. People were everywhere. I had never imagined such a thing. The atmosphere was distinctly festive. I heard that at each imperial residence the crowd of servants (*zōshiki*) and hooded women (*kinu kazuki*) was so closely-packed that it was impossible to get through. The RE apparently came out to the middle gate to watch. I gathered from him with great pleasure that he had found everything about the event and the procedure followed thoroughly worthy of a house clearly destined to endure. No doubt our household officials presented Saionji respects at each office on the way. I believe that this is my son's eighth year.

---

317 *Nichiji no kamon,* concerning the character, felicitous or otherwise, of the timing of the event.

318 Nako names six.

55
The Death of Imadegawa Sanetada

The Kikutei Grand Counselor[319] fell ill and passed away on 8.21. Having no son to succeed him, he left a wish that his younger brother, in his sixth or seventh year, should do so.[320] He died expecting that a suitable mother might yet bear him an heir, and he therefore stipulated that, should this happen, the child should in the end succeed to his house.[321] I felt very sorry for him.

---

[319] Imadegawa Sanetada, in his 25th year.
[320] Imadegawa Kiminao, Sanetada's adopted son, was actually then in his 8th year.
[321] Imadegawa Sanenao, born that year, became Kiminao's adopted son and did succeed to the house.

56
A Profession of Faith

Where there is birth, there is death. Faced with this inevitable truth I cannot help fearing the Three Evil Realms. Therefore I trust in Amida's vow—Amida who, they say, rejects no one guilty of the ten evils and the five abominations, and whose welcome is sure, should one only long truly for birth into Paradise. In that faith I have called his Name many times.

Noting the Pure Land's nine levels, [322] I leave aside the upper and middle three to consider what distinguishes the lower. When seven times seven days have passed and the lotus opens, you hear all the profound scriptures; in faith and understanding you achieve peerless aspiration; and you master for ten lesser kalpas the perfected wisdom of the hundred teachings and enter the first stage of bodhisattvahood. To hear the Three Treasures named, they say, is to achieve birth straight into Paradise (*ōjō*). It is taught that when the flower opens after twelve major kalpas within the lotus bud, Kannon and Seishi preach the truth of all dharmas and the abolition of sin, until in joy you conceive the aspiration to enlightenment. Once born into that Land you hearken to the Teaching and by degrees achieve its Fruit. I rather doubt, though, that hearing the Teaching in this life leads to freedom from birth and death in the next.

> All things pass;
> What is born dies.
> Birth and death gone,
> Quiet is bliss.[323]

---

[322] Nako's reflections on Amida's paradise seem to come mainly from preaching on the *Kanmuryōju-kyō*, which describes nine levels of birth into paradise. At the highest, the soul is born onto an open lotus throne and immediately enjoys the full presence of the Pure Land. Lower down, the soul is born into a less and less mature lotus bud, and so must wait longer and longer to enjoy that full presence. Nako sets the upper and middle levels aside out of modesty and a sense of her own unworthiness.

[323] A verse from the *Nehan-gyō* and the source of the celebrated expression *shogyō mujō* (here translated simply, "All things pass").

They call these four lines the heavenward stair of awakened aspiration; the ship bound away from the dark clouds of the passions across the ocean of love and loss; the excellent fruit of passage through the eight stages of a Buddha's life (*hassō jōdō*).

All that I have seen and heard urges me to seek release from birth-and-death. Further into these hills there is a temple named Ryōjuji.[324] Tradition has it that Kitano no Tenjin[325] roamed there of old and that the temple he knew then displayed a name plaque in his own hand. That one is gone now, and only dense greenery grew at the spot until Lord Saionji Sanekane's spiritual adviser founded this one. The Buddha's teaching has flourished there ever since.

The present abbot (*chōrō*) is known for his virtue and learning. I often take that mountain path because my late husband's remains still repose there, although properly I should reunite them with those of his forebears. I meet the abbot when I go. I once asked him, 'How am I to escape birth-and-death?' He gave me a kōan, not a word more. He never approves my attempts to answer it. Naturally I experience doubt, but working to resolve it has taught me that this is the practice most apt to sever the root of birth-and-death.

Concerted meditation is difficult amid the distractions and preoccupations that fill my day, but I cultivate mindfulness in all I do. In winter I rise, alone, to find a freezing wind beating at the window. It is a bad night. The brazier is nearly out. The bell announcing dawn starts a twinge of anguish. When will I awaken to the Real?[326]

aware kono	O that there might dawn
nemuranu toko ni	before me, at last, the Real,
miru yume o	to dispel the dreams
samasu utsutsu no	that beset me through those nights
akatsuki mo gana	sleep barely touches my eyes!

---

[324] A Rinzai Zen temple, no longer extant, founded by Musū Ryōshin.

[325] The deity name of Sugawara no Michizane (845-903).

[326] Nako remembers (1) *Shinkokinshū* 1955, in which the poet, Jakunen, laments the passage of yet another day (*kyō suginu/ inochi mo shika to/ odorokasu/ iriai no kane no/ koe zo kanashiki*); then (2) *Shinkokinshū* 1790, in which the poet, Sukezane, acknowledges that the past is a dream and laments not yet awakening to what is real (*kishikata o/ sanagara yume ni/ nashitsureba/ samuru utsutsu no/ naki zo kanashiki*).

57
In Praise of Kitayama

Within, I pursue my practice; without, I pray for the safety of my house. Praising blossoms or the moon affords one so absorbed no pleasure. Of course I yield to worldly ways and accept invitations that I cannot refuse, but such pastimes do not touch me. I feel as though I have given up the seductions of this unhappy life. In the end, though, darkness still shrouds my heart, and the mountain stream that I would gladly see clear sometimes runs troubled after all.

Nonetheless, this home of mine affords opportunities rare elsewhere to taste the pleasures of the seasons. Emperors have stayed here often. The place displays the skill of master craftsmen and remains a wonder despite its age. Trees planted reign after reign on peaks and ridges,[327] eaves glimpsed through interlaced, flowering branches, and retreat huts ranged side by side—these lovely prospects convey supreme distinction. Blossom-viewing mats spread on green moss beneath the trees lift the heart. These hills' intense autumn colors move all who see them. The stag's repeated call on the hillside deeply stirs one who lies wakeful, in tears. Flowers and leaves in season, and moonlit or snowy vistas arouse feelings beyond this world—feelings unsought, but simply what they are. The shapes of stones and trees, artless and unprompted, are all the more wonderful for being so. Pure water finds its way through rocks age after age, nor is any cupped handful ever less than pristine. Such water can banish care.

Halls (*midō*) scattered here and there further not only Saionji fortunes, since emperors commissioned them with rare piety to pray for the welfare of the realm. Generation after generation tends them

---

[327] According to *Masukagami* ("Uchino no yuki"), Saionji Kintsune, who originally acquired the Kitayama property, "decided to scatter appealing young cherry trees throughout the surrounding hills, where all the evergreens were ancient." (Perkins, *The Clear Mirror*, p. 72). Fujiwara no Teika noted in *Meigetsuki* for Gennin 2.2.8 (1225) that numerous visitors to Kitayama that month planted cherry trees there, in the spirit of *The Tale of Genji*.

with care. Of course they are many, and many, too, the associated vows to be honored, so that occasional lapses do occur. On the whole, though, these are rare.

Jōjūshin-in deserves special mention.[328] So solemn was the founding imperial vow that perpetual litanies begun there in Anjō 2.11 [1229] have continued unbroken ever since, until the present Jōwa 5 [1349].[329] Day and night, morning and evening, the chanting voices reach me through the mists of spring; or I hear through autumn fog the ringing of the altar bell. When winter gales sweep through the pines those sounds echo, in response, from the peaks, dispelling the clouds of the passions and perhaps reaching even the loftiest heavens. They still my heart.

The dedication prayer for Chōzōshin-in states, "The Saionji precincts incorporate the Four Divinities, [330] and the Buddhas frequent their holy ground. In all the realm this land is beyond compare." Yes, it is indeed of rare sanctity.

The most remote sanctum (*oku no midō*) is set aside as our final resting place. There our generations have been laid, and there voices forever call the Name. In Hongan-in,[331] forty-eight Amida Buddhas give forth their light. One may hearken there to discourses on the Pure Land scriptures or on the *Makashikan*.[332] The monks appointed to Jōkongō-in and Sanpukuji[333] are selected with great care.

---

[328] According to the *Masukagami* chapter just cited (Perkins, p. 73), Jōjūshin-in was devoted to secret rites addressed to Aizen Myōō.

[329] See the first note to no. 81 for remarks on this year, apparently the last (except for no. 85) during which Nako wrote.

[330] The divinities of the four directions: the Blue Dragon (east, flowing water), the White Tiger (west, a road), the Red Tiger (south, a basin), and the Dark Warrior (north, hills). The chapel named was within the Saionji residence complex.

[331] Another chapel within the residence complex.

[332] The great treatise by the Tendai patriarch Zhiyi (Jp. Chigi, 538-597).

[333] Both are Seizan-ha Pure Land temples, the first on the grounds of Emperor Go-Saga's Danrinji in Saga and the second in Higashiyama.

58
Sanetoshi Receives the Third Rank

The year changed to Kōei 3 [1344]. The appointments list announced his promotion to the top division (*jōkai*), and in the 3rd month he gave formal expression to his gratitude (*haiga*).[334] He received his gift (a flute, presumably in a bag) in the gentlewomen's sitting room (*daibandokoro*) at the residence of Kianmon-in. A gentlewoman brought it to him.

The first *nōshi* day[335] came that month. He wore:

nōshi, sakura	lightest pink
double *akome, moegi aya*	*moegi* green
uchiginu, kurenai	scarlet
hitoe, kurenai	scarlet
sashinuki, koki murasaki no toridasuki	dark purple
ge-kukuri, harajiro	
shita no hakama	
shaku	

---

[334] Sanetoshi, in his tenth year, has been promoted to junior third rank. According to *Entairyaku* he was added to the list (announced on 1.6) by order of Retired Emperor Kōgon.

[335] The first day of the year, imperially designated, for reporting to the palace wearing *nōshi*.

59
A Poem Exchange on Wisteria

In the midst of all these preoccupations spring came to an end. On about 5.1 I sent these, attached to wisteria in full bloom, to someone[336] who had promised but failed to visit in blossom season:

tanomete mo	You promised, you know,
towarenu hana no	but the flowers you never saw
haru kurete	are gone with the spring.
tare matsuyama to	Whose visit might they now await,
kakaru fujinami	our hills' wisteria billows?

toe ya kimi	Do please visit us,
yama hotogisu	for here the mountain cuckoo
otozurete	comes to lift his voice,
oda no sanae mo	and in the little fields nearby
torisomuru koro	they are planting seedling rice.

She replied:

tanome koshi	It is too late now
hana no sakari wa	for the visit I promised
suginuredo	then, in blossom time;
ima no kokoro ni	but these days my heart is set
kakaru fujinami	upon wisteria billows.

---

336 Perhaps the "usual old lady" of no. 66 and the "old Takatsukasa lady" of no. 84. Possibly an aunt.

hototogisu　　　　　　Now that the cuckoo
sa koso satsuki no　　claims the season for his own
ono ga koro　　　　　in this, the fifth month,
naku ya yamaji o　　　his call from your mountain paths
omoi yaritutsu　　　　echoes in my every thought.

60
Retired Emperor Kōgon Moves to a New Residence

The New Year came [Kōei 4, 1345], and the Retired Emperor repaired to his new residence.[337] The Third-Rank Counselor [Sanetoshi][338] accompanied him as his sword-bearer, wearing

kariginu, shiro ao	light *ao* green
akome, kōbai no uki-orimono	plum pink
sashinuki, koki murasaki, toridasuki	dark purple

The Sanjō-bōmon Grand Counselor[339] greeted the RE at the carriage dock (*kuruma yose*). In attendance as a Senior Noble was the Third-Rank Captain [Sanetoshi];[340] then there were four Privy Gentlemen, upper- and lower-ranking Hokumen guards, five men from the RE's secretariat (*meshitsugi-dokoro*), and twelve ox drivers. Their many *suikan* colors created an indescribable effect. Quite unusually, the RE made his journey on foot.[341]

---

[337] Kōgimon-in's newly built residence on the west side of Jimyōin House. This progress, his first of the year, took place on 3.16.

[338] Now in his eleventh year.

[339] Nakanoin Michifuyu.

[340] At the time, Sanetoshi was a captain (*chūjō*) in the Palace Guards. He was not appointed counselor (*chūnagon*) until Jōwa 5.3.25 (1349). Nako may therefore have written this entry, retrospectively, in 1349.

[341] His new residence was extremely close to his old one.

61
Kōgimon-in's Five Practices

In the 3ʳᵈ month of this year Kōgimon-in undertook the Five Practices,³⁴² apparently for her own benefit after death (*gyakushu*), thus following closely the example of Ōmiya-in.³⁴³ During the present Cloistered Emperor's [Hanazono's] reign she ranked as Mother of the Realm (*kokumo*) and so received formal imperial visits (*chōkin*).³⁴⁴ This made her the mother of *three* emperors³⁴⁵—something surely unparalleled. I gather that the Senior Nobles, and the Privy Gentlemen who scattered flowers,³⁴⁶ shone in costume and deportment and that every one of them was there. The offerings each day were beyond counting. The event involved everyone and was generally agreed to have been extremely impressive. Indeed, I took it as confirming that our world was still, after all, what it had always been and found it thoroughly reassuring. I was asked to contribute flower petals, but, scatterbrained as I am, all I could manage was one *usuyō*-lined box filled with scarlet, shaded (*susogo*), and blue petals.

Since Kōgimon-in pressed me repeatedly to attend, I gathered my courage and went after all, seating myself as inconspicuously as possible. In their heaped profusion of color the offering garments looked just like the petals. The Retired Emperor [Kōgon] came in unannounced, and despite my embarrassment I could not keep him from seeing me. I therefore entered his presence when he pointedly asked that I should do so. "I have been worrying about you," he said, "not having seen you for so long, and I am very glad to do so now."

---

³⁴² Kōgimon-in, Kōgon's mother (then in her fifty-fourth year) had renounced the world in 1336. The event described takes place at Kitayama. The "five practices" (*goshu gyō*) mentioned may be either the *goshu shōgyō* (sutra chanting, contemplation, prostration, calling the Name, and praise) or the *goshu kuyō* (daubing the body with incense [*zukō*], offering gilt altar ornaments [*keman*], burning incense [*shōkō*], offering food and drink [*onjiki*], and offering lamps [*tōmyō*].

³⁴³ Ōmiya-in (1225-1292), daughter of Saionji Saneuji, was Go-Saga's empress, and the mother of Go-Fukakusa and Kameyama.

³⁴⁴ Kōgimon-in was Hanazono's adoptive mother.

³⁴⁵ Hanazono, Kōgon, and Kōmyō, rather than Ōmiya-in's mere two.

³⁴⁶ Paper lotus petals.

However, the ceremony was about to begin. "We must talk at leisure later on," he said and took his place among the participants. Lord Chikurin-in [Kinshige] was with him. Later on he sent word that he had been delighted to see me, despite the hectic circumstances. A packet of flower petals accompanied his message. I was so overcome that I hardly knew what to do with myself.

62
A Pilgrimage to Kamo

In the 2nd month I visited the Kamo Shrines. Thick bamboo grew within a reed fence on the way from the Lower to the Upper; plum trees bloomed here and there; and warblers sang and sang enchantingly. It was all perfectly lovely. With a pang of nostalgia I remembered when long ago the Retired Emperor [Go-Fushimi], wearing *soba-tsuzuki*, noted this scene with pleasure. I came before the main sanctuary, then went on to pray before the Tanau Shrine;[347] whereupon I realized that this must be where Saigyō composed that old poem of his, *shide no namida no.*[348] Many years ago, at the time of the Miare Festival[349] a lady known as Hyōe-no-kami-no-kimi hummed *koe matsu hodo wa* while withdrawing from the Kataoka Shrine.[350] I could still see her there. It was a touching memory.

Mitsuhira[351] appeared when I was leaving and had me alight from my carriage at the Kawaraya.[352] The two-storey building and its garden had much to commend them. I was offered the sweets (*cha no ko*) that accompany tea. The head monk there, a friend of Mitsuhira, did all he could to welcome me. From there I went on to the nun's lodge,[353] where a well-filled lunch box greeted me. For that reason I did not hurry home, but instead spent there the rest of a leisurely day.

---

[347] A subsidiary sanctuary at Upper Kamo. It enshrines Futsunushi.

[348] *Gyokuyōshū* 2786.

[349] Held at Upper Kamo on the middle *uma* day of the 4th month, before the Kamo Festival proper. The festival celebrates the birth of the deity Wakeikazuchi.

[350] *Shinkokinshū* 191, by Murasaki Shikibu. Kataoka is another subsidiary sanctuary at Upper Kamo.

[351] A Kitayama household official.

[352] The shrine temple (*jingūji*) at Upper Kamo.

[353] Unknown.

63
A Pilgrimage to Iwashimizu Hachiman

In the 10th month I visited the Yawata Shrine. At dawn it began to rain, but my people assured me that it was too late now to call off the trip, so I made up my mind to go after all. The rain showed no sign of letting up. The men on horseback were soaked. We stopped at Zenpōji[354] and waited until a pause allowed us to go on to the mountain.[355] While we rested at our lodging, Yukimitsu[356] produced some beautifully filled lunch boxes and repeatedly served wine. Yōsei[357] entertained us in various ways, and that evening was quite lively.

The next day I boarded a boat that Kazuhira had ready at Mitsu no Mimaki.[358] On a smaller one he had prepared lunch boxes and so on, decorated with chrysanthemums and autumn leaves. The weather was quite unlike the previous day. There was no wind, the waves were low, and the view was lovely. I only wished I could share it with someone able to appreciate it. Meanwhile, I reached the Yodo crossing and Toba. Two gentlewomen awaited me there, sent by Kasuga no Tsubone.[359]

---

[354] The residence complex of one of the chief priestly lineages of the shrine; they had turned it into a temple.
[355] Otoko-yama, the site of Iwashimizu Hachiman.
[356] Identity uncertain.
[357] The head of the temple associated with the shrine.
[358] At Yodo in present Fushimi-ku, Kyoto, on the west bank of the Kizu-gawa.
[359] Saionji Kinmune's mother.

64
A Pilgrimage to Kasuga

In the middle of the 1ˢᵗ month[360] the Hino Counselor [Sukeaki] went on pilgrimage to Kasuga and invited me to join him. Glad of such trusted company,[361] I decided immediately to go. I started from Kitayama, which is far from Inari, and he had a long wait for me there. He had brought many of his household staff. There was one carriage for gentlewomen, and mine boarded it. I purposely brought no housemen; from Inari I sent them all back. The Kajii Prince lent me some porters.[362]

We reached the Shrine at sunset and went round the sanctuaries[363] under a brilliant moon. There was no sign of spring mist—perhaps Mikasa-yama shines too brightly for that.[364] The Deity illumined the world eight thousand years ago, they say, and I reflected in awe that that light shines, unchanged, even now.[365]

yo o terasu	You light of the world,
onaji yachiyo mo	unchanged these eight thousand years,
mikasayama	Mikasa-yama,
onaji hikari to	with the moon's own radiance
tsuki zo sayakeki	you illumine all.

---

[360] Perhaps of Kōei 4 (later, Jōwa 1), 1345.

[361] Sukeaki is her uncle.

[362] Prince Son'in, Go-Fushimi's fourth son, was the Tendai *zasu*. The porters (*rikisha*) are shaven-headed menials who shoulder palanquins, lead horses, and so on.

[363] The Kasuga Shrine has four main sanctuaries, a fifth known as the Wakamiya, and dozens of more or less prominent smaller ones. Nako would have visited them all.

[364] An allusion to *Zoku Goshūishū* 135.

[365] "Eight thousand years" presumably means simply many. Nako's conception of the deity of Mikasa-yama (i.e., the Kasuga deity) merges Amenokoyane, the divine ancestor of the Fujiwara, with Amaterasu, the source of the imperial line. According to the medieval Kasuga treatise *Shun'ya jinki*, Amaterasu acknowledged to Amenokoyane, upon emerging from the Heavenly Rock Cave, that his devotion had restored light to the world (*Kasuga* [Shintō taikei, Jinja-hen 13], Shintō Taikei Hensan Kai, 1985, p. 180). In general, Nako's thoughts and language in this section often recall such Kasuga documents as *Kasuga Gongen genki* (1309). She may even have been shown the *Genki*, to which access was rare. However, the Kasuga priests are likely to have explained shrine matters to her in similar terms.

Upon offering *mitegura* to convey my profound respect, I reflected a little further:

tanomitsutsu	A prayer in my heart,
osoremi aogu	I turn my gaze aloft in awe,
waga kata ni	and I cannot doubt
nabikazarame ya	the God's response: the streamers,
kami no yuushide	offered, fluttering my way.

Tempered light manifesting traces below (*wakō dōjin no suijaku*), benefits conferred through impartial, expedient means: I, too, I know, can count on these blessings. Enlightenment accomplished through life's eight phases (*hassō jōdō no owari*), He smiles with joy to hear offered for his pleasure (*hōraku*) the chanted wisdom of the marvelous Mahayana teaching; and they say that He answers prayers in both this life and the next.[366]

Since I was to stay the next day near Uji, I quietly visited each of the sanctuaries and also entered the halls of Tōdaiji and Kōfukuji.

Mikasa-yama

---

[366] This passage resists confident translation, but its rhetoric recalls two passages in *Kasuga Gongen genki*. The first occurs in the story of Ichiwa (scroll 8) and the second in the conclusion to the work (scroll 20). (Tyler, *The Miracles of the Kasuga Deity*, pp. 211, 291.) Nako's text appeals above all (although without consistently quoting it) to the well known line that sums up medieval syncretic thought: *wakō dōjin wa kechien no hajime, hassō jōdō wa rimotsu no owari nari*. (*Miracles* explains these words on p. 214, n. 14, but many other works in English do so as well.) In a manner consistent with the cult conveyed by Kasuga literature and art, Nako assimilates the divine presence at Kasuga to the enlightened buddhas themselves, as a collective entity summed up in Shakyamuni. *Hōraku* refers to sutra readings offered before the main Kasuga sanctuaries.

65
A Trip to Uji and Fushimi

At Uji I stayed with a friend—so I gathered—of Yasumitsu and received a warm welcome.[367] At dawn I took a boat across the river. A very chilly wind was blowing out on the water, while mist prettily veiled the view just as though, one might say, it knew that its moment had come.[368]

shibafune no	Brushwood-laden boats
watari mo miezu	cross over, invisible
kasumi komete	through thick banks of mist,
kawa oto shizumu	while the river murmurs on
uji no yamamoto	beneath the Uji hills.

When my boat rowed in to Fushimi I looked out toward the imperial residences, which called up many memories of those who had sojourned there.[369] In the moon-viewing pavilion, of old, the sun and moon were painted shining over a stormy sea, and a great mirror hung there seemed to throw back their light. All that came back to me, and it was very sad to see the place so utterly neglected. Wine went round while I surveyed the scene, until it grew too dark to see. I was sorry to leave the view behind.

---

[367] Tsuchimikado Yasumitsu, a son of Hino Sukeaki.
[368] In poetry, as in Part Three of *Genji monogatari*, mist was a stock feature of Uji and the river there.
[369] These residences were a Kami Gosho ("Upper Palace") southwest of Fushimi-yama and a Shimo Gosho ("Lower Palace") on the river. They had belonged to the Jimyōin line since Go-Fukakusa's time. Nako is probably thinking especially of Go-Fushimi.

66
The Preaching at Ryōjuji

On Jōwa 1.12.15 [1345] a preaching (*dangi*) was held at Ryōjuji. I meant to attend, but there was such heavy snow—over two feet—that I doubted being able to get there. Still, I very much wanted to, so I made up my mind to go and invited the usual old lady to come with me. The palanquin bearers had the greatest difficulty getting through. The further we went, the deeper the snow. We could not see where we were going, but we kept on anyway, since we could not get lost as long as we followed the path cut into the slope. A lot of people had gathered. I could see how determined *they* had been.

I heard a horse and assumed that it was someone else coming to join the assembly; but no, it turned out to be a messenger, Iekage, from Jimyōin House. He brought a letter from Kōgimon-in, asking about the snow. I hurried home when the preaching was over and wrote an answer. An icicle had frozen in a very curious way onto a pine branch, so I laid out some old autumn leaves prettily in a box lid, tied a pheasant to the branch, and sent the messenger off with the gift and some wine. My elderly friend composed the reply in my stead:

machi mibaya	I would love to see you.
furinishi yoyo ni	Each snowfall, reign after reign,
tachikaeri	renews those now past,
mukashi no ato mo	and each imperial call
taenu miyuki o	shows there will always be more.

Thinking it a shame not to share the gift, Kōgimon-in sent it to the Retired Emperor [Kōgon] and attached her reply to a sprig of bamboo:

kuretake no	This most noble house
yoyo ni furinishi	after snows reign after reign
yado nareba	since time out of mind,
matsu ya miyuki no	now awaits a call renewed,
ato mo tae seji	in sign of snows yet to come.[370]

---

[370] The translations of these two poems seek to convey the spirit, if not the letter, of the customary word play on *miyuki*, "imperial progress" and "snow."

67
The Death of Ōmiya Suehira

On Jōwa 2.5.25 [1346] the Ōmiya Novice, the Right Minister,[371] passed away. Such is life, of course, but it still saddened me. In the old days there was talk of having him adopt me.[372] I could not imagine that it was serious, but it was. My husband was about to ask him for my hand when conflict broke out, and I heard no more about it. For years thereafter I assumed unhappily that all the turmoil had prevented Suehira from raising the subject again.[373]

Eifukumon-in, the Kikutei Grand Counselor [Sanetada], and now this loss: I realized more sharply than before that no one lives forever.

---

[371] Suehira (1287-1346) was a son of Kinhira and an uncle of Kinmune.
[372] Presumably as a step toward her marriage to Kinmune.
[373] This discussion of marriage and adoption arrangements is difficult to interpret with confidence.

68
Spiritual Aspiration

To exist, despite disgust,[374] is our lot as human beings; to cling to life yet die is our fate. Naturally the old depart, but the young do not necessarily remain. Therefore love and affection are merely a tender moment, a fleeting intimacy. To what can one give one's heart? Where to go, not to loathe this dreary life? How to cultivate unswerving aspiration? They say that all dharmas arise from the mind. Things are good or bad in accordance with the mind. Karma bears the fruit of past deeds. Aspiration to enlightenment matures in buddhahood, greed in starving ghosts, and anger in searing fire; and beasts are stupidity. Karma is like a balance that sinks under weight. They say, though, that even a little good outweighs much evil. In effect the Wonderful Law is beyond karma. The Great Teacher's authority transcends right and wrong. How could one ever, without the power of the Law, efface grievous sin? The thing is always to cultivate studiously the One Mind.

Similarly, whether walking, standing, sitting, or lying, one should never yield in the effort to answer the kōan. Shun evil, then, and cling to the good. *Yomogi* grows straight, not crooked, when surrounded by hemp, and a vine clinging to a pine tree naturally stretches upward a thousand fathoms. So they say, and it must be true.

---

[374] *Itou to iedomo*: disgust with the evil of the profane world.

69
Kōgimon-in's Visit to Kitayama

In the 10th month of that year [Jōwa 2, 1346], the First-Rank Princess[375] paid a sudden visit to Kōgimon-in. No doubt she wanted to see the autumn leaves. Perhaps to avoid the pomp and circumstance that her visit would provoke if announced in advance, she ordered that nothing should be said about it even to her servants. Being unexpected, it caused a commotion. We had some wine, however, and Kōgimon-in remarked that that should do for the time being. "This would be rather shabby, though," she added," if by any chance she *had* let us know. The Princess presented Kōgimon-in with an inkstone, a bookrest (*bundai*), a flower vase, and an incense box (*kōbako*). From our side she received a flower vase and whatnot.

---

[375] Mitsuko Naishinnō, a daughter of Kōgon, in her twelfth year.

70
A Pilgrimage to Hatsuse

How it all began I could not say, but each morning I offered flowers and incense to the Kannon of Hatsuse. In the days of my anger against the Gods and Buddhas I rejected them all, but not this Kannon, to whom I prayed. Hatsuse was so far away, though, that I could not make up my mind to go. The months and years slipped by until in Jōwa 3.1 [1347] a sacred dream decided me on a discreet pilgrimage.

I left the capital on 1.28 and spent that night at Nara. Morotoshi arranged lodging for me in the Deer Pavilion.[376] I had a prayer to address to the Deity, so I made an offering of *mitegura* and so on. Tōbokuin[377] kindly sent wine. I set off before daybreak on a round of the sanctuaries. The sky above the hills began to lighten while I was chanting invocations (*nenju*) before the main sanctuaries. There was no one about. It was very quiet. Looking back over the past, I felt a surge of confidence that the Deity would never forsake me.

kami ya shiru	O Divinity,
hiku shimenawa no	do you in the sacred rope
uchihaete	drawn out here so long
hitosuji ni nomi	recognize a heartfelt depth
tanomu kokoro o	of longing for your blessing?

The green blinds of fivefold sole consciousness and the vermilion fence of the hundred teachings' wisdom gates, moistened by the dew of dually empty suchness gave me profound joy, and I was sorry to leave, but I had to be on my way.[378] I went round the sanctuaries before full day, then set off on my long journey.

---

[376] *Shika no yado*, unknown but clearly connected with the Kasuga Shrine.

[377] A major Kōfukuji subtemple associated with the Saionji. Saionji Sanekane's son Kakuen, a Kōfukuji superintendent (*bettō*), had resided there.

[378] The green blinds and vermilion fence evoke the main Kasuga sanctuaries. "Fivefold sole consciousness" (*gojū yuishiki*) and "dual-emptiness suchness" (*nikū shinnyo*) are Hossō terms favored by Kōfukuji, hence Kasuga. This rhetoric recalls the opening passage of *Kasuga Gongen genki* (Tyler, *Miracles*, pp. 160-164).

From where they brought me lunch I saw on a hill to the east, across the ricefields, two cryptomeria (*sugi*) trees hung with three rings, and I was struck to learn that this was hallowed Miwa-yama.[379]

At Hatsuse, the temple and its surroundings impressed me greatly, and the sweeping view from my lodging, when I paused there to rest, was quite lovely. The evening clouds roaming the sky looked almost near enough to touch, and the evening bell ringing out over the cypress woods (*hibara*) was very moving.[380]

I curtained off my space[381] and went before Kannon., whose feast day (*ennichi*) it was. The crowd was noisy.[382] I had been dedicating thirty-three Kannons to go with the main one I had honored for many years on my personal altar, and I especially wanted to do that here; so I did. I suppose I had in mind our house and all the troubles that had so long beset it, and in general my hope that it should endure safely forever, generation after generation.[383]

Kannon's expedient devices for aiding sentient beings surpass all others, and so too the sacred character of this mountain. Whoever once treads its ground, they say, is forever spared falling into the Three Evil Realms. They also say that in all Three Worlds there are only three agate plinths like the one on which Kannon apparently stands: one in India, one on Mount Fudaraku, and the one here at Hatsuse; and perhaps that is true.[384] Kannon's salvific efforts on behalf of living beings have never failed on the past, nor do they now, for the Hatsuse River runs on, its voice unceasing, and the deep hues of great

---

[379] Nako sees Miwa on her left (east) before turning eastward toward Hatsuse at what is now Sakurai. The three linked rings mentioned signify *mi* ("three") *wa* ("ring[s]"), the name of the ancient Miwa Shrine.

[380] These woods were an established *utamakura* of Miwa and Hatsuse.

[381] In the main hall, as was customary for someone going on retreat there.

[382] Kannon's *ennichi* is the 18th of the lunar month, a date that seems not to match Nako's itinerary.

[383] See no. 75, below, for more on these images of Kannon. It is unclear how many she dedicated at Hatsuse, or whether she re-dedicated there some (or all?) already dedicated elsewhere.

[384] An item in *Zoku-kyōkunshō* 13 describes the Hasedera Kannon as standing on a "vajra plinth" (*kongōza*) the like of which is otherwise to be found only in the land of Magada in Tenjiku (India), where the Buddha achieved enlightenment, and on Fudaraku-sen (Mount Potalaka), where Kannon preaches.

mercy and compassion color the trees on the hill of Yashio[385]—although such similes must still be inadequate. Worthy of trust in this present life, Kannon's expedient means toward emancipation are more trustworthy still.

The people gathered before the altar fell silent, the night wore on, and the altar lamps burned low. Peace came at last when those with me lay down and slept. A gentle rain began to fall. It stopped a while at daybreak, and I heard a chilly wind sweep down from the hills across the cypress woods. By full daylight it was pouring again, and I hurried on my round of the temple's sanctuaries. I came before the Yoki Shrine,[386] the sacred presence of Kitano no Tenjin; and the Hatsuse River I had heard so often roared as it cut around the foot of the hill. The hill was covered solely with cherry trees, while on Yashio only maples grew.[387] It was rather extraordinary to see two hills divide spring and autumn this way between them.

---

[385] Also called Yoki-yama, east of the temple across the Hatsuse River.

[386] Yoki Tenman Jinja, dedicated to the deified spirit of Sugawara no Michizane, no great distance from the temple.

[387] The difference between the two hills or knolls, Yoki and Yashio is unclear. The name Yashio seems to appear nowhere else.

71
Return to Kyoto Via Nara

On 2.1 I spent the night in Nara, then on the 2nd went on to the capital. Single cherries[388] were blooming along fences here and there, and perhaps because the spring sun shines equally on the humblest cottage,[389] so that the buds of other, more commonplace trees enjoy the same blessing, the prospect gave me, too, who matter so little, the feeling that I have much to look forward to.

I remember how, of old, Ujimitsu[390] went to the Kasuga festival as the Heir Apparent's [the future Kōgon's] envoy, and how Lady Nii[391] and I accompanied him. That, too, must have been in the 2nd month.

Since distressing incidents can occur in the vicinity of Uji,[392] I abruptly decided to spend that night in the lodge of Grand Prelate Shusen.[393] I could hear him nearby, noisily preparing to receive me and darting about as though in search of Koyurugi refreshments.[394] I was to leave first thing the next morning, but my host came forth, treated my men to wine, and spent so much time reminiscing about the old days that the sun eventually rose in the distance over Asahi-yama.[395] It might still have been dangerous to cross the Kohata hills, so I went round by way of Mitsu-no-mimaki. A meal was prepared for me there, and after a rest I went on to the capital.

---

[388] Rather than the double cherries (*yaezakura*) of Nara, mentioned in *Shikashū* 29.

[389] From *Kokinshū* 870.

[390] Nako's younger brother.

[391] Unidentified. She is probably not Ujiko (no. 30), who at the time was not yet married.

[392] *Ayashiki koto.* The issue is presumably bandits.

[393] Unidentified.

[394] An old folksong described a host rushing about to collect seaweed on "Koyorogi" (Nako reads the name a little differently) coast near present Odawara, to go with wine for his guests. Allusions to it appear also in *Kokinshū* 874 and 1094 (Azuma-uta).

[395] A hill across the Uji River from the Byōdōin.

72
The Thirteenth Anniversary of Kinmune's Death

I can hardly believe that I have heartlessly outlived him so long in this vale of tears, but thirteen autumn have come and gone. I first thought of having the Lotus Sutra formally copied and dedicated for him (*nyohōkyō*); but instead I performed the Five Practices in Hōsui-in.[396] Water sounds so mingled with the voices morning and evening chanting the Lotus Confession (*senbō*) that they might have been from waves on the Lake of the Eight Merits (*hachikudokuchi*); and the banners seemed to flutter in the cool breezes of heaven, so refreshingly did the wind murmur in the boughs. Both trees and waters might have been those of paradise. I was deeply moved.

On the second day [8.2] there was a sermon at Ryōjuji, and on the occasion I dedicated a *Kongō-kyō* copied in gold. At Hōsui-in the Five Practices ended that day, and there was another scripture dedication: a *Hōkyōin darani*[397] that I had written onto the back of a letter in *his* hand. Many ladies dedicated other things. They had sacred texts chanted as well. The officiant was the head priest of Sanpukuji.[398] I offered two clothing sets, with *hitoe-gasane* and *suzushi* robes. At Saionji there was an intensive reading of the Amida-kyō (*Amida sanmai*). Lady Nii must have arranged it.

---

[396] A chapel within the Kitayama compound, mentioned in *Masukagami*. For the Five Practices, see no. 61.
[397] A text, especially favored then in Zen, believed to help toward birth in paradise.
[398] Mentioned in no. 57: a Jōdo-shū (Seizan-ha) temple in Higashiyama.

73

The Thirty-Third Anniversary of Kinhira's Death

This year was the thirty-third after the passing of the late Chikurin-in Novice and Minister [Saionji Kinhira]. Kōgimon-in arranged the Buddhist observances, and there was a scripture dedication at Muryōkō-in. On 9.25 she and the Retired Emperor [Kōgon] arrived in a single carriage. The Senior Nobles were seated on the west and east sides of the hall, and on the eastern veranda there was a purple-bordered mat for the temple page (*dō dōji*).[399] The southernmost bay of the hall was reserved for the RE, and a brocade standing curtain was placed in the bay next to it.[400] No doubt standing curtains were also set out there for her gentlewomen. The Senior Nobles were:

> The Tōin Left Minister [Kinkata]
> The Ōmiya Grand Counselor [Kimina]
> The Director of the Heir Apparent's Household [Tōin Sanenatsu]
> The Hino Grand Counselor [Sukeaki]
> The Shijō Grand Counselor [Takakage]
> The Hamuro Counselor [Nagamitsu]
> The Shijō Consultant [Takamochi]
> The Sono Consultant [Mototaka]
> The Chikurin-in Third-Rank Captain [Sanenaga]
> The Saionji Third-Rank Captain [Sanetoshi]

I forget the others.

My Third-Rank Captain entered from the Fishing Pavilion (*tsuridono*) and took his seat to the west. The hills looked lovely in their first flush of autumn color. Pampas grass plumes nodded at the foot of the steps, water trickled among the rocks—it was all extremely pretty. The lattice shutters (*kōshi*) on the west side were raised; the lake made a flawless mirror; the setting sun beautifully gilded the Amida;[401] and the welcoming host of bodhisattvas, tossing their dancing sleeves, seemed truly present, shining, before my eyes. The Third-Rank Captain withdrew when the Confession rite was nearly over, perhaps because the

---

[399] The *dō dōji* distributed the flowers for the ceremony. On this occasion he was Fujiwara no Yasutada (*Entairyaku*).
[400] For Kōgimon-in.
[401] The Amida figure in the *raigō* scene of Amida's welcome to the departing soul.

RE decreed that since he had not yet taken part in any sacred court ritual he should not be involved in presenting the offerings. The offerings for the officiant, Chōshun, were handled by the Left Minister. The others followed in order of seating precedence, all the way down to the Privy Gentlemen. The Left Minister and the Director of the Heir Apparent's Household had a drink of wine in private. The horses and oxen were then led forth. The RE and Kōgimon-in were served wine and refreshments once the rite. The gifts for those attending (*hikidemono*) were distributed privately.

The next day, the RE visited the other temple halls. The Third-Rank Captain accompanied him as his sword-bearer, wearing

kariginu, fusenryō, ominaeshi	greenish yellow
suō no akome	maroon
koki [murasaki] sashinuki	dark purple

The RE was served a meal on his return to the main hall. He also called on the young Prince.[402] A messenger had repeatedly announced his wish to see his son, but the Prince, who had been ill, remained sufficiently unwell that a visit to his father was out of the question. Nonetheless, his father so insisted on a least a moment together that the Prince rallied his strength and came.[403] The RE called him over to where he sat. It was a memorable moment.

"I had expected to find here evidence of the ravages of time," the RE said, "but I see with surprise that the place remains unchanged and the future promises well." He continued warmly, "I have by no means forgotten the past, and I regret not having called on you for so long. I should like come back often for the pleasure of being here." The evening was over by the time he left. He spent that night at Kōgimon-in's residence and on the 27th proceeded directly to Takenaka House.[404]

---

[402] Prince Iyahito, his second son and the future Go-Kōgon.

[403] Protocol forbids Kōgon to visit Iyahito. Iyahito, born in 1338 and now in his tenth year, must come to him.

[404] Without returning to Jimyōin House. Takanaka House in Saga, where Kinhira had once lived, was Kōgimon-in's family home and at this time the residence of Kinshige.

74
First Snow in the Ninth Month

The Retired Emperor had arrived on the 25th, and on the last day of the month it snowed a little. It is very rare for the year's first snow to fall on the last day of the 9th month. I sent the wife of the Kamakura Intendant of the Right Watch [Ashikaga Tadayoshi] some autumn leaves in a box lid lined with chrysanthemum and autumn leaf-dyed *usuyō* paper:

miyuki sou	A fresh fall of snow
yado no momiji no	has graced the bright autumn leaves
yachichishio ni	around my dwelling,
kimi zo ikuyo no	dyeing them in deeper hues
iro o kasanen	in sign of long reigns to come.

She replied:

ikuyo min	How many, the reigns
kimi ga kokoro no	they will see, those autumn leaves
iro soete	colored by your heart
miyuki furinuru	in hues ever more intense
yado no momijiba	and crowned with sovereign snows?

At about that time I had occasion to send Grand Counselor Sukeaki a message. He answered, "At the moment I am watching winter rain pour from the sky:

hitoshio no	I kept watch, hoping
iro ya somuru to	to see their color deepen
miru hodo ni	just a little more;
shigure to tsurete	but then rain began to fall,
furu momiji kana	and with it the autumn leaves.

I sent straight back:

hitoshio o	Do not feel deprived
oshimu ni araji	that you missed that little more.
momijiba o	The rain you saw fall
sasoite misuru	must have meant that you should note
shigure nariken	the winter fate of autumn leaves.

One snowy morning I received a pheasant taken by a hawk and sent it to the Shiba Nun,[405] accompanied by a winecup. The Grand Counselor wrote, "The snow has just tempted me to call on her," and he replied in her stead:

washi no yama	Devoted as you are,
fukaku irinu to	I gather, to Eagle Peak,
kikishikado	such a gift as this
taka no tori tote	must rather have startled you:
miru mo mezurashi	a bird taken by a hawk.[406]

---

[405] The second wife of Sukena Nako's father, and perhaps Nako's mother.
[406] "Eagle Peak" (*washi no yama*) in this playful verse refers to Ryōjuji (nos. 56, 78, 81).

75
Dedication of an Image of Kannon

To fulfill a long-standing vow, I made an image of Eleven-Headed Kannon. The height, one foot and six inches, was modeled on that of the sixteen-foot Kannon of Hasedera. Inside the image I placed:

three Buddha-relic grains (from Tōji, handed down in our house in a crystal pagoda)

thirty-three Eleven-Headed Kannon (wood)

one scroll of the Kannon Sutra[407] (copied by me in gold characters, each written after a prostration, on the back of paper bearing the late Grand Counselor's [Kinmune's] handwriting)

I dedicated this Kannon in the Sanjin-dō[408] on Jōwa 3.12.18 [1347]. The Hōin Seien[409] officiated. In my heart I had a little prayer of my own.

---

[407] A section from the eighth scroll of the Lotus Sutra.
[408] A small hall within the Saionji residence complex.
[409] Unknown. Hōin is an ecclesiastical title.

76
A Pilgrimage to Kōzanji

At the end of the 3rd month of Jōwa 4 [1348] the Third-Rank Captain [Sanetoshi in his 14th year] made a pilgrimage to Toganoo.[410] The Prince [Iyahito],[411] being so young [11th year], mingled with the gentlewomen to accompany him. Two carriages went. The eight gentlewomen presumably wore light robes (*usuginu*) over their heads, with their skirts tucked up.[412] Mitsuhira went ahead with the children and housemen. They dismounted before the main hall and drew up the horses there in fine array.[413] The Captain first worshiped the painting (*miei*) of Kasuga, then took out the relics (*shari*).[414] He donated two robes (plum pink, lattice pattern). After visiting the other halls he rested in the Akai Lodge and received a warm welcome there.[415]

He then climbed Takao,[416] and Yukimitsu, who had brought wine, apparently served it there. The gentlewomen went straight home.[417] Mitsuhira had brought food and drink in case of need, and, not wishing to waste them, he amused himself at a temple near Hiraoka[418] with wine and a lunch box. That night he returned home by torchlight.

---

[410] The site of Kōzanji, a Shingon temple restored by Myōe Shōnin (1173-1232). Kōzanji and its Kasuga shrine were revered by the regental houses (*sekkanke*) and the Saionji.

[411] The future Go-Kōgon.

[412] *Hikiori*, i.e. *tsubo shōzoku*: normal travel dress for lady of moderate standing. Rather than allow her skirts to fall free, the wearer hitches them up under her waistband and lets the robe's excess length sag over the waistband, forming a sort of loose bag (*tsubo*).

[413] To receive Sanetoshi and the main party.

[414] *Hanazono-in shinki* (Gen'ō 2.9.8 [1320]) mentions this painting, paired with one of Sumiyoshi, and attributes both to Myōe Shōnin. The relics mentioned had probably belonged to Myōe.

[415] The Akai-no-bō ("holy water lodge") had been Myōe's residence at Kōzanji.

[416] To visit Jingoji, the temple revived by the colorful Mongaku Shōnin.

[417] Women were not allowed up Takao, the hill on which Jingoji is situated.

[418] Umegaoka in present Ukyō-ku.

77

The Thirteenth Anniversary of Go-Fushimi's Death

The thirteenth anniversary of Retired Emperor Go-Fushimi's passing came in the 4th month of that year. For Buddhist rites there were the Five Practices, performed at Jimyōin House. The Palace (*dairi*) sent flower petals. A "lake" sunk into a large gold "island"[419] bore up two boats (gold-trimmed) filled with six sets of flower petals shaded dark to light (*susogo*) in *Genji*-inspired colors, especially those worn by the ladies in the "women's concert."[420] On the island were planted gold lotuses with finely worked silk flowers.

As a personal gesture I offered the "Prediction of Destinies" chapter,[421] on red paper (dyed front and back; embroidered on a red ground with lotus blossoms and tendril motifs; bordered with lotus blossoms and tendril motifs in silver openwork; the crystal roller ends trimmed with gold openwork; the title likewise gold and silver; jeweled cord) wrapped in thin blue paper. I let Kōgimon-in know that for the occasion I had added this touch of my own to the gestures made by many others for the benefit of the departed. My offering, intentionally presented together with the sutra scroll, was ten packets of gold dust wrapped in thin paper, dyed varying shades of purple, and laid in a gold "willow box" (*yanaibako*). Kōgimon-in expressed deep gratitude for my thoughtfulness.

The dedication should properly have coincided with the sermon, but for the sutra scroll that would have been a waste since the sermon came after dark; so it was brought forward to daytime. I should have been there, but I could not make up my mind to go. I gathered from others that when the RE's secretary (*azukari*) entered with the scroll in an inkbox lid, the Senior Nobles called him to them and passed it around, whispering among themselves, although he could not hear what they were saying. When he placed it on the altar desk (*dōjō no*

---

[419] A *shima* (or *shimadai*), that is to say, a round-edged (*suhama*-shaped) surface on legs, bearing decorative rocks, trees, birds, tortoises, and so on, often presented as a gift.

[420] The *onnagaku* in the second "Wakana" chapter.

[421] The *Juryōbon* of the Lotus Sutra.

tsukue), the officiant opened it a little and clearly conveyed the donor's enduring devotion to the gentleman whom she had served all those years ago.

78
The Death of the Ryōjuji Abbot

The abbot (*chōrō*) of Ryōjuji fell ill that spring and weakened daily, until his Buddha-sun began to sink behind the mountains of Nirvana.[422] Actually, it was more like the Buddha teaching birth in non-birth and manifesting death in non-death.[423] We confused beings deeply mourned his clearly imminent extinction. At last, on 7.8, at the hour of the sheep [2 p.m.] he passed away in perfect dignity, as though falling asleep. He alone, people said, still held aloft on this mountain the lamp of the Teaching, and to me his passing seemed like the death of the Teaching itself.

Tears of grief wet the sleeves of all, clerical or lay. His disciples—monks, nuns, lay men or women—lifted their eyes in grief to the heavens and writhed, wailing, upon the ground. So it must have been when Shakyamuni passed away that spring night in the sal tree grove, like the moon vanishing behind Eagle Peak, while all of India wept. His learning extended in all directions, far and wide, illumining every recess of the Dharma. He was to everyone a rare treasure in this latter age.

I am grateful for the good karma that led me to find in him so great a friend in the Teaching. Dull as I am, though, at sunrise I expect sunset, in the evening I expect morning. Meanwhile time passes, the years come and go, and I have seen off five springs without achieving anything worthwhile; and now my teacher is gone. I rue past failings, but present regret changes nothing. Whatever I may have wished were otherwise, it is too late now.

---

[422] An image from the *Nehan-gyō*.

[423] A passage from *Hokke mongu*, a record of the sermons of the Tendai patriarch Zhiyi, quoted also in the first scroll of *Hōnen Shōnin eden*. The Buddha lives eternally, but he manifests birth and death in order to guide sentient beings.

79
Emperor Kōmyō Visits Jimyōin House

In the 9th month of that year His Majesty [Kōmyō] made a progress to Jimyōin House. The Third-Rank Captain [Sanetoshi] accompanied him. He had spent a long time mastering care of the Sword and Jewel. The next month the throne was to pass (*kuni yuzuri*) to a new sovereign [Sukō], and everything was done beautifully because it was his last progress there. Horses, saddles, the grooms' costumes—everyone, I heard, eagerly did their best. The Retired Emperor [Kōgon] watched from his carriage. Responsibility for the Sword and Jewel imposed demands complex enough to confuse even someone well practiced, and the prospect worried me, but nothing went wrong. In fact, people felt that His Majesty's dignity had been served particularly well. I gathered from various sources that the Commander[424] was impressed. Both Imperial Persons[425] were loud in their praise, which made the event fortunate indeed.

---

[424] Saionji Kinshige (right commander at the time) or perhaps Kasanoin Nagasada, appointed commander two months later.
[425] *Gosho gosho*: Kōgon and Kōgimon-in.

80
The Accession of Emperor Sukō and the Death of Hanazono

The accession (*senso*) took place in the 10th month [1348]. The Prince proceeded to Nijō House.[426] The Senior Nobles and Privy Gentlemen moved from there to Jimyōin House, since an Heir Apparent[427] was appointed there the same day.

After these happy events, I learned in the 11th month that the Cloistered Emperor [Hanazono] had passed away. Both Retired Emperors [Kōgon, Kōmyō] seemed to mourn him deeply.

---

[426] The residence of Nijō Yoshimoto, the regent, at Oshikōji-Karasumaru. There Prince Okihito came of age before succeeding immediately to the throne as Emperor Sukō.
[427] Prince Naohito, a son of Hanazono.

81
A Zen Retreat

Another New Year came.[428] I went to Ryōjuji as usual but found it greatly changed. The press of people had vanished, and the path there was overgrown. I recalled the passage, "Bamboo grows thick on the old path to Mount Keisoku, and of travelers there is no sign. No one any longer inhabits Kodoku Park."[429] Truly, "on Eagle Peak he had proclaimed his teaching..."[430] It was so sad!

There are meditation huts below Shinmeiji,[431] and on the 2nd I went there for a special retreat. That night I was up, alone, when suddenly rain beat on my window; not for long, though, because soon the moon shone in from above the hills to keep me company. The wind off the peaks rattled the door and helped to keep me awake. All this certainly spurred me on, but all I managed was to change where I sat. I felt so ashamed, so inadequate. Apart from my effort to try harder, nothing happened. Later, I moved to the hut to the south and sat there with the others. We all did our best to keep one another from falling asleep.

At daybreak I returned to the hut to the north. Mist hung everywhere, and nothing stood out but the fragrance of plum blossoms at the eaves.[432] The dawn sky was lovely, and a forlorn moon lingered among the clouds.

---

[428] The year is now Jōwa 5 (1349), the year to which Nako dated no. 57. In chronological order, the entries from that year are as follows:

> 1.5: latter part of no. 83 (Sanetoshi's appointment)
> 1.29: first part of no. 83 (Kōgon and Kōmyō's visit to Kitayama)
> Late 2nd or early 3rd: no. 84
> 7.13: no. 82

[429] A near-quotation from the preface to Book Two of *Sanbō ekotoba*. Keisoku is where the Buddha's disciple Kashō died. Kodokuon is another name for Gion, the site of Gion Shōja.

[430] Source as above. The characters for Washi-no-mine ("Vulture [or Eagle] Peak") also form the name of Ryōjuji. The *Sanbō ekotoba* text continues, evoking the Buddha's death, "In the Crane Grove his voice fell silent."

[431] A temple mentioned in the *kotobagaki* to *Shūishū* 502 and in *Konjaku monogatari shū* 12/35, but otherwise unknown. It must have been close to Ryōjuji.

[432] An allusion to *Fūgashū* 80.

yamakage ya	In the mountain's lee,
sugi no iori no	the first glimmer of dawn breaks
akegata ni	above my cedar hut,
kokorobosoku mo	and the moon comes forth at last,
izuru tsukikage	shedding a mournful light.

The brushwood fence along the garden path looked so flimsy that I wondered with some emotion that it alone should separate me from the profane world.[433]

aware nari	I can but wonder,
shiba no iori no	when the flimsy brushwood fence
shiba no kaki	around my brushwood hut
ukiyo no naka no	alone, I now realize,
hedate to omoeba	wards off the world's miseries.

   I could not spend the rest of my life there, though, and I was preparing to leave when heavy snow fell, too deep to get through, so I stayed on that day. The abbot to whom I looked for light after his illustrious predecessor's passing managed to get through the snow to call on me, on his way elsewhere. I was very glad to see him, but at the same time I could not help remembering the past. If only he had been, instead, the master I used to know, his slightest remark would have given me joy.

---

[433] An allusion to *Fūgashū* 1772.

82
Offerings at the Hino Graves

On 7.13 I went to the Hino subtemple (*tatchū*),[434] chanted darani and sutras, and did all I could for the benefit of the departed. It was moving to do so. Offering water for the first time to my father's father,[435] I saw the dew that forms briefly on the lotus leaf and longed especially that it might light his way through the darkness.

mayouran	Illumine the path
yamiji o terase	he must wander through darkness,
nori no mizu	Water of the Law,
musubu hachisu no	with the light shed by the dew
tsuyu no hikari ni	gathered on the lotus leaf.

---

[434] An Amida-dō at Hōkaiji in present Fushimi-ku, Kyoto, responsible for the Hino graves. It survives unchanged from Nako's time.
[435] Hino Toshimitsu.

83

An Imperial Pilgrimage to Kitayama
Sanetoshi Appointed Counselor

In Jōwa 5.1 [1349], the Senior [Kōgon] and Junior [Kōmyō] Retired Emperors made their first joint visit to our hills. The decision seems to have been made on the spur of the moment, and I protested repeatedly that it would make things difficult here; but this was the Junior's first excursion since abdicating, he had in any case no suitable residence of his own, and moreover he insisted that his visit would honor our house. So there was no escape. I provided clothing for them, hung on racks.

For the Senior:

> [kariginu], nukishiro, neri-usumono, karabana karatori
> double robe, shijira-aya, kiku hachiyō pattern
> hitoe, shijira-aya, tōbishi
> sashinuki, shijira-aya
> shita no hakama

For the Junior:

> kariginu, hana yamabuki with kyōyō and karakusa motifs
> double robe, moegi, shijira-aya; chrysanthemum and karakusa
> hitoe, white shijira-aya, hishi
> sashinuki, usuiro; toridasuki
> shita no hakama, kurenai
> harajiro usumurasaki

The novice Norikata hung these things on the racks. Both gentlemen received the same sash and fan.

Their carriage drew up to the green sliding doors (ao shōji).[436] The Senior RE wore a plain silk, light grey nōshi, no doubt because he was in mourning for the late Cloistered Emperor [Hanazono]. Lady Sanmi[437] was the gentlewoman who accompanied them in their carriage. Those in the display carriage (Tōdainagon no Sanmi-dono, Shin Hyōe-no-kami-no-Tsubone, Gonchūnagon-no-Tsubone, Daini-no-Tsubone) wore fivefold sets (itsutsuginu). Mats were laid along the south front of the main house. Within the north-facing standing curtain they were

---

[436] The private reception room in the Kitayama south pavilion.
[437] Hideko, later Yōrokumon-in.

daimon-bordered.[438] For a reigning emperor's visit the border would have been *ungen*.

Both REs enjoyed wine in private. Their own attendants and Privy Gentlemen brought it in, and gentlewomen served it from the room to the west. The Senior Nobles seated themselves in the gentlewomen's sitting room, where the Third-Rank Captain [Sanetoshi] served them wine. After the customary three cups they appeared, as summoned, before the REs (*kariginu, shō-kukuri*). Each RE received an ox and a horse, which they inspected after nightfall. Privy Gentlemen led them.

Repeated messages then let me know that they were now ready to see me. They assured me at length that the day had moved them greatly because in all ways it had brought back the past, and that henceforth they would visit often. I presented the gentlewomen with two measures of paper.[439]

That year's spring appointments list promoted the Third-Rank Captain to Counselor. This was a direct appointment (*jikinin*). He did not serve first as a Consultant.

---

[438] A bold-patterned (*daimon*) *kōrai-beri* mat border, suitable for a regent or above.
[439] "Measure" translates *ma*—apparently a unit, but now unknown.

84
Blossom-Viewing in the Rain

While receiving a little treatment in the capital that spring, I had a wonderfully pleasant talk with the old Takatsukasa lady.[440] She was so sorry to see me leave for home that she accompanied me. At Muryōkō-in the trees were in full bloom. Unable to get enough of them, we spent the day gazing at them and pouring each other wine. Then it set in to rain. Her people urged her to waste no time starting back to the city. "The mountain paths are becoming very treacherous," they said. So we gave up our blossom-viewing. From her I received:

shitaimishi	Do you realize
yamaji no hana no	how much of my heart I left
ko no moto ni	underneath the trees
tomeshi kokoro no	blooming on that mountain path
hodo wa shirazu ya	where at last you and I met.
nareshi yori	Since we became close
kakaru wakare no	I have understood full well
aran to wa	that one day we two
omoinagara mo	would end up parting like this;
nao zo odoroku	and yet I am still amazed.
nagori omou	I miss you so much,
namida no ame no	the rain of my falling tears
kakikurete	darkens all I see,
hana mo shioreshi	and the very flowers droop
kaerusa zo uki	on my sad journey home.

[440] Probably Nako's aunt, mentioned in nos. 59 and 66. She was a former dame of staff to Fushimi, a daughter of Toshimitsu, and the wife of Takatsukasa Iemasa. The intense emotion of this meeting suggests the possibility that Nako announced to her friend her intention to renounce the world. This step would not have kept the two from meeting, but it would have greatly changed the character of their relationship.

I added to my reply:

omoiyare	Just imagine, then,
ame mo namida mo	how rain and streaming tears
kakikurete	darken all I see
nagori shioreshi	and how, underneath these trees,
hana no ko no moto	the blossoms wilt with regret.
ito semete	Such was the pain
akanu nagori no	of having to let you go
kanashisa ni	that I almost wish,
nareshi sae uki	close as we have been so long,
urami to zo naru	that I had never known you.

85
Closing Poems[441]

moshiogusa	Seaweed traceries
kakite atsumuru	gathered lifelong from the brush,
itazura ni	these careless follies
ukiyo o wataru	even so have borne a nun
ama no susami ni	across the ordeals of life.
naki ato ni	Will I leave a name
uki na ya tomen	unworthy of memory
kakisutsuru	if these seawrack lines
ura no mokuzu no	cast away upon the shore
chirinokorinaba	somehow, nonetheless, survive?

---

[441] Nako wrote these poems as a nun, probably in about 1351 or 1352, that is to say, during the Kannō Anarchy. Poetry and associated writing were traditionally evoked with seaweed imagery, and sea or seashore motifs were closely linked because *ama* ("nun") also means someone who makes a living from the sea (fishing, saltmaking, diving for seaweed or abalone).

CHRONOLOGY, 1333

Nako's last palace service (Shōkyō 2.1.12) to her move to Kitayama

From Iwasa, *Zenchūshaku*, pp. 90-92

Date	Section	
1.12	(27)	Setsubun; the Blue Roans; Kōgon's directional taboo move.
1.13	(27, 26)	First day of spring. Nako leaves palace at dawn. Kinmune goes to her home that night.
1.15		Kinmune's third night with Nako. Presumably the *tokoro-arawashi* (daylight disclosure of the marriage) followed.
1.16	(27)	Women's dance (*onna tōka*) canceled because of battle in Kawachi between Rokuhara and Kusunoki Masashige.
1.18	(29)	Gift to Go-Fushimi at Tokiwai House. (Conjectural date.)
1.20		Turmoil in the city. Kinmune and Nako on duty at Tokiwai House.
1.20+	(28)	Calm returns. Nako and Kinmune sometimes meet, sometimes fail.
Early int. 2		Nako becomes unwell.
2.20+	(29)	Nako recovers. On duty at Tokiwai House
2.24		Go-Daigo escapes from Oki.
2.25		Akamatsu forces enter Kyoto, lose to Rokuhara, retreat.
3.12	(30)	Akamatsu forces defeat Rokuhara, enter Kyoto. Kōgon and two REs move to Rokuhara. Nako joins them. (Nako gives date as 16th.)
3.13	(31)	Kinmune sends Kiyokage to inquire after Nako.
3.?	(31)	Sukena moves to Kiyomizu, then Nako.
4.20+	(31)	Kinmune visits her.
4.27		Takauji, at Shinohara Hachiman, raises troops against the Hōjō.
5.5	(32)	Sweetflag (*ayame*) exchange with Kinmune.
5.7	(33)	Kōgon, Go-Fushimi, Hanazono, and heir apparent flee eastward accompanied by Sukena. Kinmune returns to Kitayama.
5.9	(34)	Kōgon and his party captured at Banba.
5.10	(33)	Nako moves to Myōōn-dō at Kitayama.
5.17		Go-Daigo deposes Kōgon and changes era to Genkō.
5.22		Kamakura Bakufu falls.

5.28	(34)	Kōgon and others return to Kyoto (Nako dates return to 27).
Mid-6	(35)	Nako moves to main house as Kinmune's formal wife (*seishitsu*).

CHRONOLOGY, 1333-1337
From Iwasa, *Zenchūshaku*, pp. 121-123

1333

Genkō 3.6.5	Go-Daigo returns to capital.
Genkō 3.6.26	Retired Emperor Go-Fushimi renounces the world.
Genkō 3.8.5	Takauji receives third rank, junior grade.

1334

Genkō 4.1.29	Era name changed to Kenmu.
Kenmu 1.6	Discord between Prince Moriyoshi and Takauji.
Kenmu 1.1.15	Moriyoshi banished to Kamakura.

1335

Kenmu 2.6.22	Kinmune and others arrested.
Kenmu 2.6.27	Kinshige becomes Saionji head.
Kenmu 2.7	Hōjō Tokiyuki attacks Kamakura. Tadayoshi kills Moriyoshi.
Kenmu 2.8.2	Kinmune and Ujimitsu executed.
Kenmu 2.8.19	Takauji defeats Tokiyuki and enters Kamakura.
Kenmu 2.9	Go-Daigo orders Takauji back to Kyoto. Takauji does not respond.
Kenmu 2.int10?	Nako gives birth to Sanetoshi.
Kenmu 2.11.19	Go-Daigo orders Nitta Yoshisada to suppress Takauji.
Kenmu 2.11.22	Retired Emperor Hanazono renounces the world.
Kenmu 2.11.26	Go-Daigo dismisses Takauji.
Kenmu 2.12.12	Takauji defeats Yoshisada at Hakone.

1336

Kenmu 3.1.10	Go-Daigo flees to Ōmi Sakamoto.
Kenmu 3.1.11	Takauji enters capital, fights Go-Daigo forces.
Kenmu 3.1.29	Defeated, Takauji retreats to Tanba.
Kenmu 3.2.2	Takauji sails from Hyōgo.
Kenmu 3.2.20	Takauji reaches Akama-ga-seki.
Kenmu 3.2.25	Kōgimon-in renounces the world.
Kenmu 3.2.29	Era name formally changed to Engen, but Ashikaga and Northern Court retain Kenmu.

Kenmu 3 [Engen 1] 3.2	Takauji defeats Kikuchi Taketoshi at Tadarahama and seizes Kyushu.
Kenmu 3 [Engen 1] 4.3	Takauji leaves Dazaifu.
Kenmu 3 [Engen 1] 4.6	Death of Go-Fushimi.
Kenmu 3 [Engen 1] 5.25	Takauji defeats Yoshisada and Kusunoki Masashige at Minatogawa.
Kenmu 3 [Engen 1] 5.27	Go-Daigo flees to Enryakuji.
Kenmu 3 [Engen 1] 5.29	Takauji enters Kyoto. Kōgon entrusts government to him. Era name changed back to Kenmu. Battles and fires in Kyoto. Kōgon to Iwashimizu and Tōji.
Kenmu 3.8.15	Go-Fushimi's third son, Yutahito, becomes Kōgon's adopted son. Genbuku and accession as Kōmyō.
Kenmu 3.10.10	Go-Daigo returns to Kyoto from Enryakuji.
Kenmu 3.12.21	Go-Daigo flees to Yoshino.

1337

Kenmu 4.3.6	Fall of Kanegasaki fortress in Echizen. Suicide of Takayoshi.
Kenmu 4.12.21	First entry in second book of *Takemuki-ga-ki*.
Kenmu 4.12.28	Enthronement of Kōmyō.

aka(iro) 赤　red

akome 衵　a robe, generally lined, worn between the *uwagi* and the undergarment

ao(ki) 青　*ao* green, a slightly bluish green

aya 綾　damask

chishio 千入　"dipped a thousand times" in the dye bath, for color intensity

ebizome 葡萄染　grape (reddish) purple

eboshi 烏帽子　The headgear normally worn by an adult man. There were several variants.

ei 纓　the pendent "tail" sometimes worn, hanging or rolled, with an eboshi

enuimono 絵縫物　a garment with embroidered motifs

fusekumi 伏組　a triple-braided cord

fusenryō 浮線綾　twill weave with pattern woven in relief

ge-kukuri 下括　tying a garment (*hakama, sashinuki, nōshi*) low, at the ankles

gyotai no hako 魚袋の筥　an ornamental leather box, decorated with fish motifs, attached to the waist of the *sokutai*: gold for third rank and above, silver for fourth or fifth rank.

hada kosode 肌小袖　a *kosode* worn as undergarment, against the skin.

hagi 萩　fabric with *ao* green warp and *suō* maroon weft. As a *kasane*, the same over *ao* green.

hakama 袴　pleated trousers

hakubai 白梅　"white plum": a white-over-pink layering

haku no gohō 帛の御袍　a white silk cloak worn by the emperor during kami rituals

hanada 縹　blue

hana yamabuki 花山吹　(see yamabuki.)

harajiro 腹白　an ornamental way of tying the *heiken* cord, especially appropriate for a boy

heiken 平絹　an ornamental cord used to tie up the *sashinuki*

heirei eboshi 平礼　a pliable, thinly lacquered *eboshi*

hiki nōshi 引直衣　imperial dress: a long-skirted *nōshi* for formal occasions

hishi 菱　woven lozenge pattern

hitatare 直垂　the straight garment favored especially by warriors; worn with *hakama*

hitoe 単　an unlined, open-sleeved garment, worn as an undergarment under the *itsutsuginu*

hitoe-gasane 単襲　two *hitoe*, worn one over the other

hō 袍　a formal outer garment worn over a courtier's *sokutai*

hyōmon 平文　a damask-weave pattern

itsutsuginu 五衣　fivefold set of robes

jizuri 地摺　stencil-dyed

joboku 如木　a heavily starched *kariginu* of white hemp cloth

kaifu 海賦　seashore motif (*mo*)

kameishi-datami 亀石畳 a textile pattern of tiled tortoiseshell shapes

ka ni arare 窠に霰 a complex textile pattern that combines a "hail" (*arare*) checkerboard pattern with a motif that resembles the cross section of a cucumber; typically occurs on a woman's *mo*

karabana karatori 唐花唐鳥 relief-woven birds and flowers

karaginu 唐衣 a lady's outermost, half-length robe

karakusa 唐草 a decorative vine motif.

karaori relief-patterned brocade

karaorimono 唐織物 an elaborately relief-patterned brocade garment

kariginu 狩衣 a man's "hunting" robe, relatively informal

kataorimono 固織物 a "stiff weave" garment: a *katajiaya* that has been dyed in the fiber rather than after weaving; named for being a rather stiff fabric—a three harness twill ground with pattern in six harness twill, usually woven with unglossed silk

kazashi 挿頭 artificial flowers set in the hair

kazami 汗衫 a girl's light outer robe

kiku hachiyō 菊八葉 eight-petaled chrysanthemum pattern

kinjiki 禁色 a *hō* 袍 color allowed only to a man of the very highest rank: for example, *kikujin*, *aka*, *ōdan*, dark *murasaki*.

kinran 金襴 supplementary patterning with gold thread (gold leaf on paper) weft

kisuji shirosuji 黄筋白筋 yellow and white horizontal stripes

kō 香 light orange

ko-aoi no aya 小葵の綾 *ko-aoi* damask: blue-green with a small, damask-weave, floral lozenge pattern

kōbai 紅梅 plum pink

kōbai no nioi 紅梅の匂 shaded plum pink

kōburi 冠 a man's formal head-dress

koji 巾子 snood: an upright envelope for the bound hair (*motodori*) under an *eboshi*. The pendant *ei*, projecting back from the base of the *koji*, would have been rolled and bound with white silk.

kōri-gasane 氷襲 ice layering: glossy white over white

koromo 衣 inner robe

kosode 小袖 an undergarment

kouchiki 小桂 a woman's relatively informal outer robe, somewhat shorter than the *uchiki*

kuchiba 朽葉 (color) warm tan

kuchiba 朽葉 (layering) tan over yellow

kurenai 紅 safflower scarlet

kyōyō (or **gyōyō**) 杏葉 apricot-leaf motif

matsu-dasuki 松襷 (unidentified)

matsugasane 松重 a layering: *suō*, over lighter *suō*, over *moegi* green, over lighter *moegi*, over still lighter *moegi*; worn with a scarlet *hitoe*.

mittsu akome 三つ袙 triple *akome* set

mittsuginu 三つ衣 triple set of robes

mittsu onzo 三つ御衣 triple set of *uchiki*

mo 裳 train worn by a gentle-woman on duty

moegi 萌葱　grass green

momiji-gasane 紅葉襲　"autumn leaf" layering (fabric or paper): *aka* over *suō*

monoimi 物忌　a hair tie of cut paper used in kami rituals (*shinji*).

mo no koshi 裳の腰　a long, ornamental sash worn with the *mo*. The sash that actually tied the *mo* on was much shorter.

mumon 無文　unpatterned

murasaki 紫　purple

murasaki no nioi 紫の匂　a layering: dark purple over five lighter and lighter purple layers; worn with a scarlet *hitoe*

murasaki no usuyō 紫薄様　three *murasaki* layers, each one lighter, over two white layers; worn with white *hitoe*

neri-usumono 練薄物　glossed thin silk

nōshi 直衣　the relatively informal, daily costume for a gentleman in court service

nukishiro 緯白　fabric woven with purple warp and white weft

obi 帯　sash

omigoromo 小忌衣　white ritual robes decorated with plants and birds in *yama-ai* green.

ominaeshi 女郎花　fabric woven with *ao* green warp and yellow weft

orimono 織物　a garment with a woven pattern

ra 羅　plain-weave silk gauze

raifuku 礼服　Chinese-style ceremonial wear reserved for the enthronement ritual

sashinuki 指貫　trousers bound at the ankles (*ge-kukuri*) or just below the knees (*shō-kukuri*)

shaku 笏　a flat length of wood about a foot long, slightly tapering and with rounded ends, that a court official held vertically before him when in formal posture

shijira-aya 繊綾　a warp-stripe twill weave

shiro 白　white

shiro ao 白青　light *ao* green

shiro orimono 白織物　a white garment with a woven pattern

shita-gasane 下襲　a ceremonial train worn under the *hō* of the *sokutai*, so that it trailed out behind

shita no hakama 下の袴　under-*hakama* (see *ue no hakama*)

shō-kukuri 上括　tying a garment (*hakama*, *sashinuki*, *nōshi*) high, just below the knees

soba-tsuzuki 傍続　relatively informal wear for a retired emperor or other such exalted person. It consisted of a *konōshi* 小直衣, i.e. a *kariginu* with a *ran* 襴 attached—a *ran* being sort of band that extended the length of the garment.

sōbu no nioi 菖蒲の匂　"sweet flag" layering: *ao* green over dark plum pink

sokutai 束帯　a gentlemen's formal costume when in court service

sugi no yokome no ōgi 杉の横目の扇　a fan with ribs of slant-grained cryptomeria

suikan 水干　a type of upper garment originally worn by men among the common people and local officials, but adopted in elaborate, ornamented form as festive or dance dress or for boys or young men. The skirts of the *suikan* were tucked into the waistband of the *hakama*.

tama no on-kōburi 玉の御冠, also *benkan* 冕冠:　"sun-jewel headdress," the emperor's ceremonial headdress, decorated with a sun disk and pendent jewels

suō 蘇方 maroon: dye from heart-wood of the sappanwood tree

susogo 裾濃 shaded downward, light to dark

suzushi 生絹 thin, somewhat stiff, unglossed, plain-weave silk

tatōgami 畳紙 general-purpose paper kept ready for various uses in the fold of one's robe

tōbishi 遠菱 a floating lozenge pattern

toridasuki 鳥襷 a weaving pattern

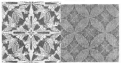

tsubomi kōbai 蕾紅梅 a layering: *kōbai* (plum pink) over *ebizome* (grape purple) or light maroon (*suō*). As an *itsutsuginu* set: five *suō*-lined *kōbai* robes worn with an *ao* green *hitoe*.

tsurubishi 鶴菱 a woven pattern of two cranes, their wings forming a lozenge

uchibakama 打袴 (see *hakama*)

uchiginu 打絹 beaten silk

uchiginu 打衣 a lined inner robe of glossed silk

uchiki 袿 a inner robe worn over the *hitoe* and under the *koromo*; or, under less formal circumstances,

worn as the outer layer of a woman's costume

ue no hakama 上の袴 over-*hakama*, worn over the *shita no hakama*; normally white, lined with scarlet.

ukiori(mono) うき織物 fabric with a pattern woven in relief

ume-gasane 梅襲 an *itsutsuginu* set: three *kōbai* (plum pink) layers, lighter to darker; one *kurenai* (safflower scarlet); and one *suō* (maroon)

unohana 卯花 a layering: white over green *or* white over white, with a white *hitoe*

uragiku 裏菊 an *itsutsuginu* set: two white over one yellow and two *ao* green

urakoki suō 裏濃き蘇方 a *suō* garment lined with darker *suō*

urayamabuki 裏山吹 a mustard-yellow *karaginu* with woven patterns in a different color weft—in this case probably red on mustard yellow, or vice-versa

usuginu 薄衣 or **usu-onzo** 薄御衣 light dress, apparently thinner and lighter than *uchiki*

usumono (see *ra*)

usumurasaki 薄紫 light purple

usuyō 薄様 thin paper

usuyō 薄様 as textile, meaning unknown: perhaps a kind of thin silk, or perhaps refers to a light purple color

usuiro 薄色 light purple

usumono 薄物 a thin silk, "gauze" or "crossed warp" weave

uwagi 表着 a full-length over-robe

uwazashi 上刺 ornamental band around the top of the *hakama*

yama-ai green 山藍 the green of the *yama-ai* plant was probably rubbed (stenciled) on, since dip-dyeing with *yama-ai* had generally fallen out of use by Nako's time

yamabuki 山吹 a mid-gold-yellow; or a fabric woven with scarlet warp and yellow weft

yamabuki 山吹 (also **hana yamabuki**) a layering: *ochiba* (light tan) over *ki* (yellow), sometimes layered also with white; worn with an *ao* green *hitoe*

yanagi 柳 willow: a fabric woven with white warp and green weft

yanagi 柳 an *itsutsuginu* set: five *yanagi* layers, worn with a scarlet *hitoe*

yanagi sakura 柳桜 lightest pink (*sakura*) lined with *usuiro* (lightest purple)

TRANSLATED OFFICIAL TITLES

These translations are based where possible on those in the Penguin *Tale of Genji*.

Acting... *gon* 権
Acting Commissioner *gon no daibu* 権大夫
Adviser *jijū* 侍従
Captain (in the Palace Guards) *chūjō* 中将
Chamberlain *kurōdo* 蔵人
Chamberlain Captain *tō no chūjō* 頭中将
Chancellor *daijōdaijin* 太政大臣
Cloistered Emperor *hōō* 法皇
Consultant *saishō* 宰相
Consultant Captain *saishō chūjō* 宰相中将
Controller *ben* 弁
Counselor *chūnagon* 中納言
Counselor Captain *chūnagon chūjō* 中納言中将
Dame of Staff *naishi no suke* 典侍
Deputy Director of the Heir Apparent's Household *tōgū no suke* 春宮亮
Director of the Heir Apparent's Household *tōgū no daibu* 春宮大夫
Director of Palace Maintenance *kamon no kami* 掃部頭
Director of the Office of Carpentry *moku no kami* 木工頭
Grand Counselor *dainagon* 大納言
Grand Prelate *sōjō* 僧正
Head Chamberlain *kurōdo no tō* 蔵人頭
Heir Apparent *tōgū* 春宮
Intendant of the Right Watch *uhyōe no kami* 右兵衛督
Junior Retired Emperor 新院
Staff Lady *naishi* 内侍
Lady of the Blood *joō* 女王 or 女皇
Left Captain *sachūjō* 左中将
Left Gate Watch Officer *saemon no suke* 左衛門佐
Left Minister *sadaijin* 左大臣
Left Grand Controller *sadaiben* 左大弁
Lord of Civil Affairs *jibukyō* 治部卿

Palace Minister *naidaijin* 内大臣

Privy Gentlemen *tenjōbito* 殿上人

Regent *kanpaku* 関白

Retired Emperor 院

Right Captain *uchūjō* 右中将

Right City Commissioner *ukyō no daibu* 右京大夫

Right Commander *udaishō* 右大将

Right Gate Watch Intendant *uhyōe no kami* 右兵衛督

Right Grand Controller *udaiben* 右大弁

Right Minister *udaijin* 右大臣

WORKS CITED

Arntzen, Sonja. *The Kagerō Diary*. Ann Arbor: Center for Japanese Studies, The University of Michigan, 1997.

Brazell, Karen, tr. *The Confessions of Lady Nijō*. Stanford University Press, 1973.

Conlan, Thomas D. *From Sovereign to Symbol: An Age of Ritual Determinism in Fourteenth-Century Japan.* Oxford University Press, 2011.

Imazeki Toshiko. *Kana nikki bungaku ron*. Kasama Shoin, 2013.

Inukai Kiyoshi, ed. *Kagerō nikki* (Shinchō Nihon koten shūsei). Shinchōsha, 1982.

Itō Kei. *Shinhokuchō no hito to bungaku.* Miyai Shoten (Miyai sensho 6), 1979.

Iwasa Miyoko, *Takemuki-ga-ki zenchūshaku.* Kasama Shoin, 2011.

Kasagi engi. In *Shugendō shiryō shū II* (Sangaku shūkyō shi kenkyū sōsho, vol. 18), edited by Gorai Shigeru. Meicho Shuppan, 1984.

Kasuga (Shintō taikei, Jinja-hen 13). Edited by Shintō Taikei Hensan Kai. Shintō Taikei Hensan Kai, 1985.

Keene, Donald. *Seeds in the Heart.* New York: Henry Holt, 1993.

Mostow, Joshua S. and Royall Tyler. *The Ise Stories.* University of Hawai'i Press, 2010.

Nara-ken no chimei (Nihon rekishi chimei daijiten 30). Heibonsha, 1981.

Ogawa Takeo. "Hokuchō teishin to shite no *Masukagami* no sakusha: seiritsu nendai, sakuzō no saikentō." *Mita Bungaku* 32 (September 2000).

Perkins, George W. *The Clear Mirror: A Chronicle of the Japanese Court During the Kamakura Period (1185-1333).* Stanford University Press, 1998.

Pigeot, Jacqueline. *Mémoires d'une éphémère (954-974)*. Paris: Collège de France, Institut des Hautes Études Japonaises, 2006.

Stavros, Matthew, with Norika Kurioka. "Imperial Progress to the Muromachi Palace, 1381: A Study and Annotated Translation of *Sakayuku hana*." *Japan Review* 28 (2015).

Tonomura, Hitomi. "Re-envisioning Women in the Post-Kamakura Age." In Jeffrey P. Mass ed., *The Origins of Japan's Medieval World: Courtiers, Clerics, Warriors, and Peasants in the Fourteenth Century*, Stanford University Press, 1997.

Tyler, Royall. *The Miracles of the Kasuga Deity*. Columbia University Press, 1990.

————, tr. *The Tale of Genji*. Viking, 2001.

Wakita Haruko, trans. Alison Tokita. *Women in Medieval Japan: Motherhood, Household Management and Sexuality*. Clayton: Monash Asia Institute, 2006.

REFERENCE WORKS ON COSTUME AND COLOR

Nagasaki Seiki. *Kasane no irome*. Kyoto: Kyōto Shoin, 1988.

Hachijō Tadamoto. *Subarashii shōzoku no sekai*. Seibundō Shinkōsha, 2005.

Imperial House

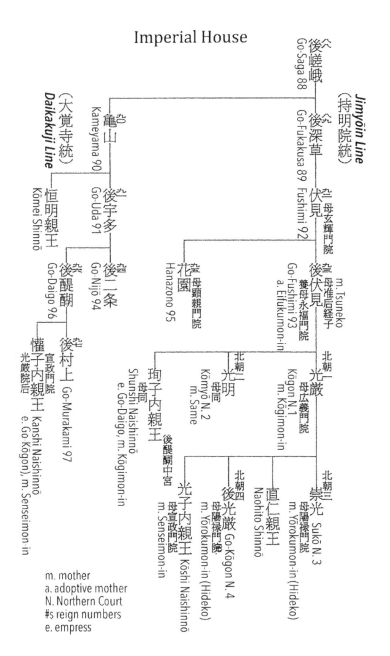

Jimyōin Line (持明院統)

Daikakuji Line (大覚寺統)

後嵯峨 Go-Saga 88

後深草 Go-Fukakusa 89

亀山 Kameyama 90

恒明親王 Kōmei Shinnō

後宇多 Go-Uda 91

伏見 Fushimi 92　母玄輝門院

後二条 Go-Nijō 94

後醍醐 Go-Daigo 96

後醍醐 Go-Daigo 96

花園 Hanazono 95　母顕親門院

後伏見 Go-Fushimi 93　養母永福門院　a. Eifukumon-in

m. Tsuneko 母准后経子

光厳 北朝一 Kōgon N.1　母広義門院　m. Kōgimon-in

懌子内親王 宣政門院　光厳院后　Kanshi Naishinnō　e. Go-Kōgon), m. Senseimon-in

後村上 Go-Murakami 97

珣子内親王 母同 Shunshi Naishinnō　e. Go-Daigo, m. Kōgimon-in　後醍醐中宮

光明 北朝二 Kōmyō N.2　母同　m. Same

光子内親王 Kōshi Naishinnō　m. Senseimon-in

後光厳 北朝四 Go-Kōgon N.4　母陽禄門院　m. Yorokumon-in (Hideko)

直仁親王 Naohito Shinnō

崇光 北朝三 Sukō N.3　母陽禄門院　m. Yorokumon-in (Hideko)

m. mother
a. adoptive mother
N. Northern Court
#s reign numbers
e. empress

These four genealogical charts are adapted from Iwasa, *Zenchūshaku*, pp. 314-316.

Hino House

(with relationships to the Ashikaga shoguns)

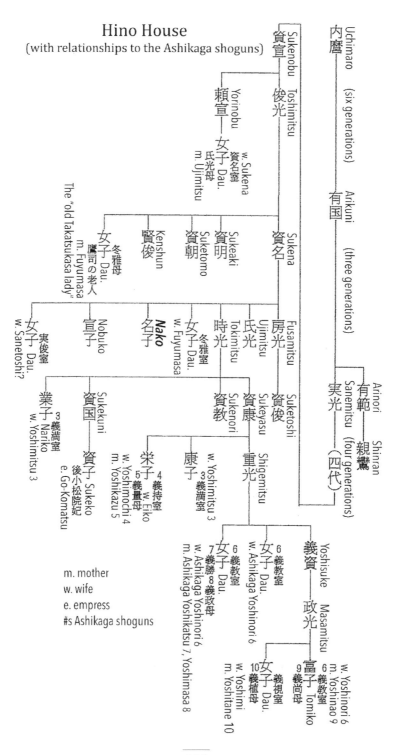

m. mother
w. wife
e. empress
#s Ashikaga shoguns

185

Saionji House

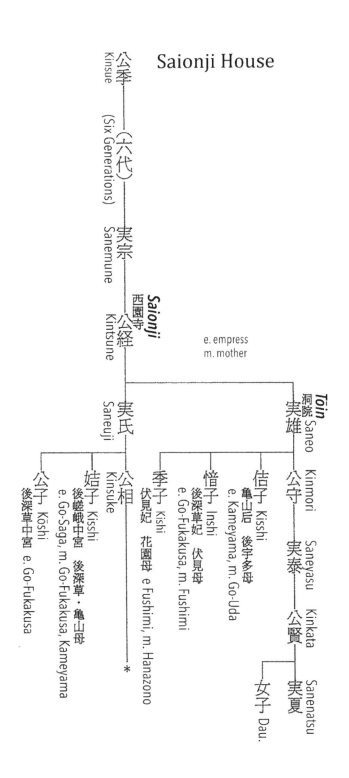

e. empress
m. mother

Saionji House
Kinsuke's line

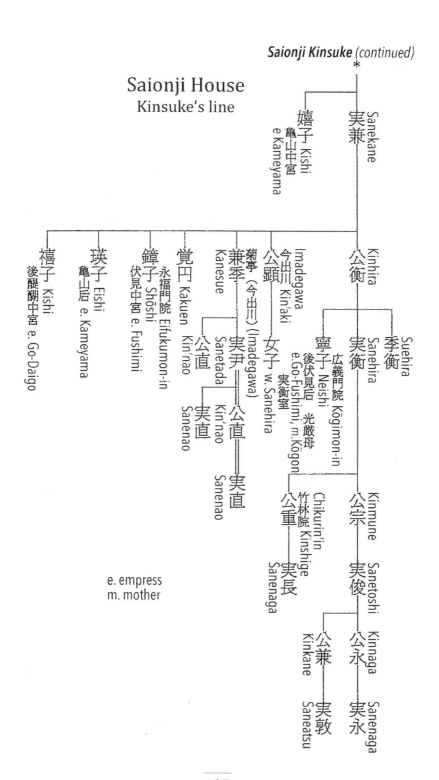

e. empress
m. mother

実兼 Sanekane

嬉子 Kishi 亀山中宮 e Kameyama

公衡 Kinhira

禧子 Kishi 後醍醐中宮 e. Go-Daigo

瑛子 Eishi 亀山后 e. Kameyama

鏱子 Shōshi 伏見中宮 e. Fushimi

覚円 Kakuen

兼季 Kanesue

菊亭 (今出川) (Imadegawa)

公顕 Kin'aki

今出川 Imadegawa Kin'aki

女子 w. Sanehira

寧子 Neishi 広義門院 Kōgimon-in 後伏見后 e.Go-Fushimi, m.Kōgon

光厳母 m. Kōgon

公衡 Kinhira

実衡 Sanehira

季衡 Suehira

公直 Kin'nao

実尹 Sanetada

実衡室 実衡室

公重 Chikurin'in 竹林院 Kinshige

実長 Sanenaga

実直 Sanenao

公直 Kin'nao

実直 Sanenao

公宗 Kinmune

実俊 Sanetoshi

実永 Sanenaga

公永 Kinnaga

公兼 Kinkane

実敦 Saneatsu

Made in United States
Troutdale, OR
08/11/2023

11979840R00121